973.o1
S
Snow, Dean R.

The Archaeology of North

973.01
S
Snow, Dean R.

AUTHOR

The Archaeology of North
TITLE America.

$16.95

DATE DUE	BORROWER'S NAME
4-25-89	Joyce Burke
3-20-90	Mike McKenna
	Mrs. Burke
MAY 05 '92	Gene L.3P

THE
ARCHAEOLOGY
OF
NORTH AMERICA

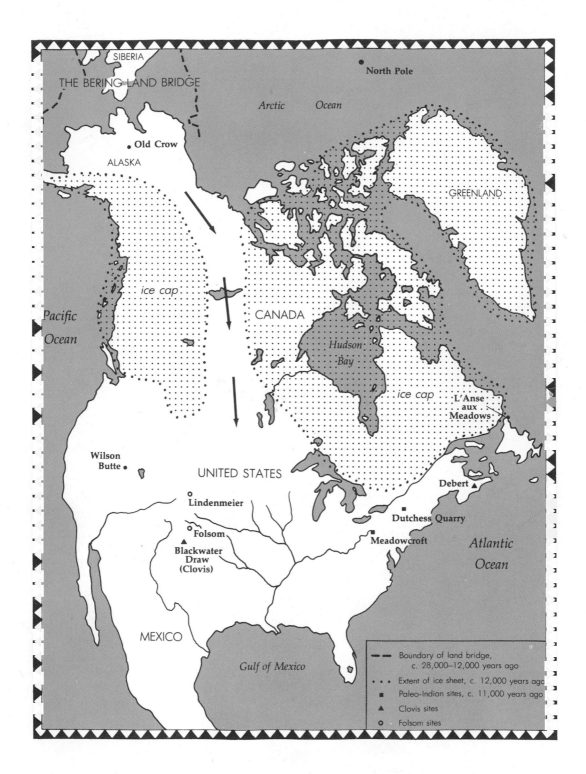

SIBERIA

THE BERING LAND BRIDGE

North Pole

Arctic   Ocean

Old Crow

ALASKA

GREENLAND

*Pacific
Ocean*

ice cap

CANADA

*Hudson
Bay*

ice cap

L'Anse
aux
Meadows

Wilson
Butte

UNITED STATES

Debert

Lindenmeier

Dutchess Quarry

Folsom

Meadowcroft

*Atlantic
Ocean*

Blackwater
Draw
(Clovis)

MEXICO

Gulf of Mexico

– – – Boundary of land bridge,
          c. 28,000–12,000 years ago

• • • Extent of ice sheet, c. 12,000 years ago

■ Paleo-Indian sites, c. 11,000 years ago

▲ Clovis sites

○ Folsom sites

THE ARCHAEOLOGY OF NORTH AMERICA

Dean R. Snow
State University of New York at Albany

Frank W. Porter III
General Editor

CHELSEA HOUSE PUBLISHERS
New York   Philadelphia

On the cover Head-shaped pottery, Mississippian tradition, probably representing a war trophy.

Chelsea House Publishers
Editor-in-Chief Nancy Toff
Executive Editor Remmel T. Nunn
Managing Editor Karyn Gullen Browne
Copy Chief Juliann Barbato
Picture Editor Adrian G. Allen
Art Director Maria Epes
Manufacturing Manager Gerald Levine

Indians of North America
Senior Editor Marjorie P. K. Weiser

Staff for **THE ARCHAEOLOGY OF NORTH AMERICA**
Copy Editor Karen Hammonds
Deputy Copy Chief Ellen Scordato
Editorial Assistant Claire M. Wilson
Assistant Art Director Laurie Jewell
Picture Researcher Kim Dramer
Production Coordinator Joseph Romano

First Printing

1 3 5 7 9 8 6 4 2

Library of Congress Cataloging-in-Publication Data

Snow, Dean R., 1940–
The Archaeology of North America / by Dean Snow.
    p. cm.—(Indians of North America)
Bibliography: p.
Includes index.
Summary: Discusses the origins of America's Indians, their myths, and their culture in various regions of the continent up to the time of the conquest.
ISBN 1-55546-691-5
      0-7910-0353-1 (pbk.)
1. Indians of North America—Antiquities. 2. United States—Antiquities. [1. Indians of North America—Antiquities.]
I. Title. II. Series: Indians of North America (Chelsea House Publishers)   88-18120
E77.9.S57 1989   CIP
973'.01—dc 19   AC

CONTENTS

INDIANS OF NORTH AMERICA

CHELSEA HOUSE PUBLISHERS

INDIANS OF NORTH AMERICA: CONFLICT AND SURVIVAL

Frank W. Porter III

The Indians survived our open intention of wiping them out, and since the tide turned they have even weathered our good intentions toward them, which can be much more deadly.

John Steinbeck
America and Americans

When Europeans first reached the North American continent, they found hundreds of tribes occupying a vast and rich country. The newcomers quickly recognized the wealth of natural resources. They were not, however, so quick or willing to recognize the spiritual, cultural, and intellectual riches of the people they called Indians.

The Indians of North America examines the problems that develop when people with different cultures come together. For American Indians, the consequences of their interaction with non-Indian people have been both productive and tragic. The Europeans believed they had "discovered" a "New World," but their religious bigotry, cultural bias, and materialistic world view kept them from appreciating and understanding the people who lived in it. All too often they attempted to change the way of life of the indigenous people. The Spanish conquistadores wanted the Indians as a source of labor. The Christian missionaries, many of whom were English, viewed them as potential converts. French traders and trappers used the Indians as a means to obtain pelts. As Francis Parkman, the 19th-century historian, stated, "Spanish civilization crushed the Indian; English civilization scorned and neglected him; French civilization embraced and cherished him."

Nearly 500 years later, many people think of American Indians as curious vestiges of a distant past, waging a futile war to survive in a Space Age society. Even today, our understanding of the history and culture of American Indians is too often derived from unsympathetic, culturally biased, and inaccurate reports. The American Indian, described and portrayed in thousands of movies, television programs, books, articles, and government studies, has either been raised to the status of the "noble savage" or disparaged as the "wild Indian" who resisted the westward expansion of the American frontier.

Where in this popular view are the real Indians, the human beings and communities whose ancestors can be traced back to ice-age hunters? Where are the creative and indomitable people whose sophisticated technologies used the natural resources to ensure their survival, whose military skill might even have prevented European settlement of North America if not for devastating epidemics and the disruption of the ecology? Where are the men and women who are today diligently struggling to assert their legal rights and express once again the value of their heritage?

The various Indian tribes of North America, like people everywhere, have a history that includes population expansion, adaptation to a range of regional environments, trade across wide networks, internal strife, and warfare. This was the reality. Europeans justified their conquests, however, by creating a mythical image of the New World and its native people. In this myth, the New World was a virgin land, waiting for the Europeans. The arrival of Christopher Columbus ended a timeless primitiveness for the original inhabitants.

Also part of this myth was the debate over the origins of the American Indians. Fantastic and diverse answers were proposed by the early explorers, missionaries, and settlers. Some thought that the Indians were descended from the Ten Lost Tribes of Israel, others that they were descended from inhabitants of the lost continent of Atlantis. One writer suggested that the Indians had reached North America in another Noah's ark.

A later myth, perpetrated by many historians, focused on the relentless persecution during the past five centuries until only a scattering of these "primitive" people remained to be herded onto reservations. This view fails to chronicle the overt and covert ways in which the Indians successfully coped with the intruders.

All of these myths presented one-sided interpretations that ignored the complexity of European and American events and policies. All left serious questions unanswered. What were the origins of the American Indians? Where did they come from? How and when did they get to the New World? What was their life—their culture—really like?

In the late 1800s, anthropologists and archaeologists in the Smithsonian Institution's newly created Bureau of American Ethnology in Washington, D. C., began to study scientifically the history and culture of the Indians of North America. They were motivated by an honest belief that the Indians were on the verge of extinction and that along with them would vanish their languages, religious beliefs, technology, myths, and legends. These men and women went out to visit, study, and record data from as many Indian communities as possible before this information was forever lost.

8

By this time there was a new myth in the national consciousness. American Indians existed as figures in the American past. They had performed a historical mission. They had challenged white settlers who trekked across the continent. Once conquered, however, they were supposed to accept graciously the way of life of their conquerors.

The reality again was different. American Indians resisted both actively and passively. They refused to lose their unique identity, to be assimilated into white society. Many whites viewed the Indians not only as members of a conquered nation but also as "inferior" and "unequal." The rights of the Indians could be expanded, contracted, or modified as the conquerors saw fit. In every generation, white society asked itself what to do with the American Indians. Their answers have resulted in the twists and turns of federal Indian policy.

There were two general approaches. One way was to raise the Indians to a "higher level" by "civilizing" them. Zealous missionaries considered it their Christian duty to elevate the Indian through conversion and scanty education. The other approach was to ignore the Indians until they disappeared under pressure from the ever-expanding white society. The myth of the "vanishing Indian" gave stronger support to the latter option, helping to justify the taking of the Indians' land.

Prior to the end of the 18th century, there was no national policy on Indians simply because the American nation had not yet come into existence. American Indians similarly did not possess a political or social unity with which to confront the various Europeans. They were not homogeneous. Rather, they were loosely formed bands and tribes, speaking nearly 300 languages and thousands of dialects. The collective identity felt by Indians today is a result of their common experiences of defeat and/or mistreatment at the hands of whites.

During the colonial period, the British crown did not have a coordinated policy toward the Indians of North America. Specific tribes (most notably the Iroquois and the Cherokee) became military and political pawns used by both the crown and the individual colonies. The success of the American Revolution brought no immediate change. When the United States acquired new territory from France and Mexico in the early 19th century, the federal government wanted to open this land to settlement by homesteaders. But the Indian tribes that lived on this land had signed treaties with European governments assuring their title to the land. Now the United States assumed legal responsibility for honoring these treaties.

At first, President Thomas Jefferson believed that the Louisiana Purchase contained sufficient land for both the Indians and the white population.

Within a generation, though, it became clear that the Indians would not be allowed to remain. In the 1830s the federal government began to coerce the eastern tribes to sign treaties agreeing to relinquish their ancestral land and move west of the Mississippi River. Whenever these negotiations failed, President Andrew Jackson used the military to remove the Indians. The southeastern tribes, promised food and transportation during their removal to the West, were instead forced to walk the "Trail of Tears." More than 4,000 men, women, and children died during this forced march. The "removal policy" was successful in opening the land to homesteaders, but it created enormous hardships for the Indians.

By 1871 most of the tribes in the United States had signed treaties ceding most or all of their ancestral land in exchange for reservations and welfare. The treaty terms were intended to bind both parties for all time. But in the General Allotment Act of 1887, the federal government changed its policy again. Now the goal was to make tribal members into individual landowners and farmers, encouraging their absorption into white society. This policy was advantageous to whites who were eager to acquire Indian land, but it proved disastrous for the Indians. One hundred thirty-eight million acres of reservation land were subdivided into tracts of 160, 80, or as little as 40 acres, and allotted to tribe members on an individual basis. Land owned in this way was said to have "trust status" and could not be sold. But the surplus land—all Indian land not allotted to individuals— was opened (for sale) to white settlers. Ultimately, more than 90 million acres of land were taken from the Indians by legal and illegal means.

The resulting loss of land was a catastrophe for the Indians. It was necessary to make it illegal for Indians to sell their land to non-Indians. The Indian Reorganization Act of 1934 officially ended the allotment period. Tribes that voted to accept the provisions of this act were reorganized, and an effort was made to purchase land within preexisting reservations to restore an adequate land base.

Ten years later, in 1944, federal Indian policy again shifted. Now the federal government wanted to get out of the "Indian business." In 1953 an act of Congress named specific tribes whose trust status was to be ended "at the earliest possible time." This new law enabled the United States to end unilaterally, whether the Indians wished it or not, the special status that protected the land in Indian tribal reservations. In the 1950s federal Indian policy was to transfer federal responsibility and jurisdiction to state governments, encourage the physical relocation of Indian peoples from reservations to urban areas, and hasten the termination, or extinction, of tribes.

Between 1954 and 1962 Congress passed specific laws authorizing the termination of more than 100 tribal groups. The stated purpose of the termination policy was to ensure the full and complete integration of Indians into American society. However, there is a less benign way to interpret this legislation. Even as termination was being discussed in Congress, 133 separate bills were introduced to permit the transfer of trust land ownership from Indians to non-Indians.

With the Johnson administration in the 1960s the federal government began to reject termination. In the 1970s yet another Indian policy emerged. Known as "self-determination," it favored keeping the protective role of the federal government while increasing tribal participation in, and control of, important areas of local government. In 1983 President Reagan, in a policy statement on Indian affairs, restated the unique "government to government" relationship of the United States with the Indians. However, federal programs since then have moved toward transferring Indian affairs to individual states, which have long desired to gain control of Indian land and resources.

As long as American Indians retain power, land, and resources that are coveted by the states and the federal government, there will continue to be a "clash of cultures," and the issues will be contested in the courts, Congress, the White House, and even in the international human rights community. To give all Americans a greater comprehension of the issues and conflicts involving American Indians today is a major goal of this series. These issues are not easily understood, nor can these conflicts be readily resolved. The study of North American Indian history and culture is a necessary and important step toward that comprehension. All Americans must learn the history of the relations between the Indians and the federal government, recognize the unique legal status of the Indians, and understand the heritage and cultures of the Indians of North America.

An archaeologist directs a team of students digging at the Klock site in upstate New York, where remains of a late prehistoric Mohawk village have been found.

DISCOVERING AMERICAN INDIAN ORIGINS

This is a book about the origins of the Indians of North America. It is also about the science of archaeology, the only way in which we can discover those origins. Archaeology is the systematic recovery of objects and other material evidence for human existence in the past and the study of that evidence.

The Indians north of Mexico had no writing before the arrival of Europeans. Written records exist only for a few recent centuries, and these documents are the province of historians. Archaeologists have the task of investigating the thousands of years of Indian prehistory that came before written records. Furthermore, although life in North America was recorded in documents from 1492, when Christopher Columbus and his crew landed on an island in the Caribbean, archaeology is needed to supplement the scanty written documentation.

Written documents for periods prior to 1492 are scarce even for Europe and Asia, especially in comparison with the mountains of documents produced in our own century. The requirements of government and commerce were much simpler in the European Middle Ages than they are today. The world that most people knew was relatively unchanging. Few could read or write; typesetting, which made inexpensive books possible, was a new invention in the late 15th century. The conditions of the times also contributed to the lack of documents: Most people did not have the leisure to pursue an interest in their own histories, and few even suspected the existence of other cultures. Knowledge of the familiar world was to be found in a small number of ancient religious writings to which only specialists had access.

All that changed with the scientific discoveries and explorations of the Renaissance in the 15th and 16th centuries. The world was not flat after all, and there were whole continents out there that could not be accounted for by traditional religious beliefs. Exciting new discoveries by explorers and the rediscovery of ancient writings dealing with mathematics and science prompted people to reexamine the past. They read classical Greek and Latin texts of all kinds with new interest. They undertook archaeological excavations in order to recover the monuments and inscriptions that would substantiate these texts. Thus, in Europe, the practice of archaeology developed to help make sense of this rediscovered history.

By the 19th century both Europeans and Americans were extending archaeological investigations to their own backyards. Europeans could discover their own pasts through archaeology, but Americans could find evidence only of past American Indian cultures. The Virginia lawyer and future president Thomas Jefferson was among the first to carry out careful archaeological excavation in America. Jefferson excavated a burial mound near his home in Virginia and wrote a thorough description of those Indian graves that is still useful today.

Archaeology began as a means to illuminate history, and at first that meant the history of art and architecture. However, as time went on archaeology began to shed light on other aspects of history, such as events narrated in Greek and Latin texts. As archaeology took on the characteristics of historical science, so too did geology and biology. The findings of these sciences often contradicted long-held popular beliefs, and these contradictions often brought scientists into prolonged conflict with many people who could not accept the new ideas, and especially with practitioners of organized religions.

Experimental sciences can verify their conclusions through repetition of experiments, but historical sciences seek to explain long-term processes from evidence that often appears as a series of complicated one-time events. Nevertheless, the historical sciences depend on the same principles of logic and proof as other sciences. It took a long time to overcome traditional beliefs and convince people that the earth circled the sun. It has also taken a long time to convince most people that dinosaurs had evolved and become extinct before human beings existed, that human beings themselves evolved from much earlier primate ancestors, and that American Indians came to the Western Hemisphere from Asia only after humans had evolved to their modern form. Scientists continue to argue about many details of these events. But there is no controversy at all among scientists about the basic underlying principles or the broad developments in biological and cultural evolution.

This book presents what archaeologists now know about the prehistory of the Indians of North America, their way of life before the arrival of Europeans and before the time for which we have written documentation. There are many uncertainties and disagreements over the details of North American prehistory. Our present understanding

Exhuming the First American Mastodon, *painted by Charles Willson Peale in 1806. In 1801, Peale had led family members and friends in a New Jersey dig where they unearthed two skeletons that they called "mammoths," which were later exhibited in the museum that Peale had established in Philadelphia in 1785 and in the one that his son Rembrandt would later open in Baltimore.*

will surely be modified as time goes on and the science of archaeology advances. About the most basic and fundamental principles, however, it is unlikely that there will be any significant change in our thinking. Beyond the fundamentals, archaeologists and other scholars agree that there is much we do not yet know, as well as much about what we have already learned that we do not yet fully understand. To all scientists, uncertainty is a welcome challenge, for it sets the stage for tomorrow's discoveries. Archaeologists particularly love uncertainty, for every discovery is a challenging mix of ancient data and new interpretation at the same time.

Mundus nouus.

ALBERICVS VESPVTIVS LAVRENTIO
PETRI DE MEDICIS SALVTEM PLVRI
MAM DICIT.

Uperioribus diebus satis ample tibi scripsi de reditu meo
ab nouis illis regionibus:quas & classe:& impensis:et man
dato isti? serenissimi portugaliæ regis perquisiuimus:et in
uenimus:qua sq nouum mundum appellare licet. Quando
apð maiores nostros nulla de ipsis fuerit habita cognitio
& audientibus omnibus sit nouissima res. Etenim hec opi
nionem nostrorum antiquorum excedit:cum illorum maior pars dicat vl
tra lineam equinoctialem:& versus meridiem non esse continentem:sed ma
re tantum quod atlanticum vocare:et siqui earum continentem ibi esse af
firmauerunt:eam esse terram habitabilem multis rationibus negauerunt.
Sed hanc eorum opinionem esse falsam:et veritati omnino cõtrariam hec
mea vltima nauigatio declarauit: cũ in partibus illis meridianis contine
rem inuenerim frequentioribus populis: et animalibus habitatam:q̃ no
stram Europam:seu Asiam:vel Africam: et insuper aerem magis tempera
tum et amenium: q̃ in quauis alia regione a nobis cognita: prout inferius
intelliges:vbi succicte tantum rerum capita scribemus:et res digniores an
notatione :et memoria:quæ a me vel visæ:vel audite in hoc nouo mundo
fuere:vt infra patebit.

Prospero cursu quartadecima mensis Mai) Millesimoquingentesimo
primo recessimus ab Olysippo mandante præfato rege cum tribus na
uibus ad inquirendas nouas regiones versus austrum Uiginti mensibus
continenter nauigauimus ad meridiem: Cuius nauigationis ordo talis est
Nauigatio nostra fuit per insulas fortunatas:sic olim dictas:nunc autē
appellantur insulæ magnæ canariæ:quæ sunt in tertio climate: et in confi
bus habitati occidentis. Inde per oceanum totum littus africum:et par
tem ethiopici percurrimus vsq ad promontorii ethiopum:sic a prolomeo
dictũ:quod nunc a nostris appellatur Caput viride: et ab ethiopicis Bese
gbice. et regio illa mandinga gradibus 14. intra torridam zonam a linea
equinoctiali versus Septentrionem:quæ a nigris gentibus et populis habi
tatur. Ibi resumptis viribus: et necessarijs nostræ nauigationi et tulimus
ancboras:et expandimus vela ventis: et nostrum iter per vastissimũ occa
num dirigentes versus antarticbum parumper per occidentem inflexim?

Amerigo Vespucci, the Italian navigator who made three voyages to Central and South America between 1499 and 1502, was the author of Mundus novus (The New World), *one of his few writings. It appeared as an appendix to* Cosmographiae Introductio *by Martin Waldseemüller, the 1507 book that first used the geographical designation* America, *derived from Vespucci's given name.*

In 19th-century Europe, interest in local prehistory led archaeology to develop independently of other sciences. In North America, Americans whose own ancestors had come largely from Europe and Africa became interested in local prehistory and contemporary American Indian cultures at about the same time. Thus in the United States and Canada it was natural for ethnologists, people who studied the ways of life of living peoples, to become closely allied with archaeologists. This led American anthropology to develop as a scholarly discipline combining archaeology, ethnology, linguistics (which involves the study of languages), and physical anthropology (which involves the study of human biology).

In the United States and Canada today, archaeologists pursue either of two somewhat different traditions. Classical archaeologists obtain degrees in Classics, the study of Greece and Rome, the ancient civilizations of the Mediterranean. Archaeologists whose work focuses on North America generally have degrees in anthropology, although some Canadian archaeologists follow the British tradition of earning a degree specifically in archaeology.

The earliest European explorers of the Americas thought they had found the eastern edge of Asia. Accordingly, they called the people they came upon "Indians," and the name stuck. North and South America were named—almost by accident—after the Italian navigator Amerigo Vespucci, who was not the first European to arrive and did not deserve the honor. He had explored the coast of South America in 1499 and 1501 and recognized it as a new continent. So both parts of the term "American Indian" are incorrect—and the product of European myths. Even the names given to specific tribes or nations often come from nicknames, simple errors, or popular myths. Nevertheless, we must use the terms that are likely to be most clearly understood by the largest number of readers, pointing out their mythical origins when necessary.

Professional archaeologists have traditionally given proper credit to the Indian cultures responsible for the sites and artifacts found across America, but this has not always been true of the writers and readers of popular accounts of American archaeology. In fact, popular archaeology has often strayed far from reality, attributing Indian finds to non-Indian civilizations, because of prejudices that are connected to its European heritage.

The transplanted Europeans who settled the United States and Canada tended to deny that American Indians could have been responsible for build-ing the prehistoric monuments that still dot the landscape of the Eastern Woodlands. Thus in the 19th century the burial and temple mounds, impressive earth constructions found in Ohio and elsewhere in the East, were not attributed to Indians. It became popular to assume that the moundbuilders had been a superior race of non-Indians who had only recently been replaced by Indians. Many people found this easy to believe because at the time the Indians often lived in small, scattered, and seemingly uncivilized communities. What most people of the 19th century did not know was that most Indian nations had suffered devastating population losses 200 to 300 years earlier as a result of diseases brought to the Americas by Europeans. Furthermore, 200 years of warfare had turned many

Moundville, Alabama, an example of earthen pyramids that resemble Mexican temple structures.

MOUND DIGGERS

American archaeology owes a great debt to two early 19th-century Ohioans, Ephraim George Squier and Edwin Hamilton Davis. Squier, a newspaper editor and amateur archaeologist, and Davis, who provided funding as well as his presence, carefully surveyed the earthen mounds of the Ohio Valley. They pursued their interest in the mounds with sober judgment and tireless care. They avoided the temptation of rash speculation and concentrated on describing monuments that even then were disappearing as a result of farming and construction. They traveled hundreds of miles across the Eastern Woodlands at a time when travel was very difficult, excavated some 200 sites, and recorded their findings with detailed maps, careful drawings, and thorough descriptions. In 1846 they presented their findings in a lecture to the American Ethnological Society. In 1848 their book *Ancient Monuments of the Mississippi Valley* was the first volume issued by the recently founded Smithsonian Institution. Little would be known today about many important sites without their work. By sticking to facts and pressing the search despite difficulties, Squier and Davis earned the permanent respect of future archaeologists.

Serpent Mound, Ohio, built 2,000 years ago, is nearly half a kilometer (about two-thirds of a mile) long. The serpent's head is too far away to be seen.

of the survivors into poor refugees. The Indians of the 19th century were survivors of several centuries of almost continual disruption of their culture.

But the American settlers of European descent did not know this. Their bias toward their own civilization led them to decide that, if the moundbuilders had been a superior people, they must have originated in Europe. This idea appealed to those who felt that otherwise they had no roots in America. Gradually, stories about European visits and migrations to America before the time of Columbus were introduced by popular writers. These tales have persisted into the late 20th century, even as archaeology has developed and our understanding of American Indian prehistory has increased.

Occasionally a popular myth has some basis in fact. In 1837 a scholar named Carl Rafn set off the first cycle of the Viking myth when he asked Americans to look for evidence of Viking (Norse) visits to North America. Old Scandinavian sagas strongly suggested that there had been visits to Greenland and to the east coast of North America. Americans, especially those of Scandinavian descent, loved the idea, and rushed off to look for evidence. Of course, when people are intent on finding evidence it turns up everywhere. The enthusiasm turned ordinary things into Viking artifacts in the popular imagination. Holes in rocks on the East Coast became mooring holes for Viking ships. An old mill in Rhode Island became a Viking castle. An In-

The Kensington Runestone in west central Minnesota was carved in the late 19th century. It was a fraud that fooled many people into believing it was evidence for prehistoric visits by Vikings to Minnesota. This replica, made in 1951, is five times the size of the original.

dian buried with a sheet of copper became a Viking in full armor. Discarded farm implements became Viking weapons.

The enthusiasm for Vikings even led to several frauds. The most famous of these was the Kensington Runestone, a rock allegedly inscribed with an old Norse text, which turned up in a region of Scandinavian-American settlement in Minnesota. The runestone inscription fooled several enthusiasts into spending their lifetime trying to prove that the Norse had explored Minnesota long before later Scandinavians immigrated there in the 19th century. As is often the case in such matters, professional archaeologists who called the inscription a fake were seen as killjoys and were challenged to prove that the stone was not authentic. (This is, of course, contrary to standard scientific procedure.) We now know that the Kensington Runestone was carved as a prank around 1885 by a person whose knowledge of both runic inscriptions and geography was so poor that only those who had a reason to believe it could have done so.

In more recent decades careful archaeological research has shown that there were indeed two long-lived Norse settlements on the coast of Greenland. In addition, in 1960 the Scandinavian archaeologist Helge Ingstad discovered the site of L'Anse aux Meadows near the northern tip of Newfoundland. This site was apparently built and lived in by Norse colonists around 1000 A.D. More recently a coin of Norse origin turned up in a collection from a site on the coast of Maine. Today books based on competent archaeology often sit next to what is left over from the nonsense of past Viking fads on the shelves of public libraries.

In recent years, the idea of early Celtic settlers has supplanted interest in the Vikings. Some popular writers have claimed that these people, the ancestors of the modern Irish and Welsh, crossed the Atlantic long before Columbus. The New England soil is rocky, and farmers there have long used local stones to build fences, animal pens, house foundations, storage cellars, ovens, and other ordinary structures. Many farms of the early New England settlers were abandoned for better land when people moved west, and it is not uncommon to find old stone walls and other structures in woods that have regrown over the last hundred years. These structures have provided much excitement for people with imagination and a desire to find evidence of prehistoric Celts in America. A site in New Hampshire known as Mystery Hill is just an unusual old farmstead, but you can pay admission there to see a supposed Celtic sacrificial stone and other mysterious structures. You can see a nearly identical stone and find out how it was made and used by New England farmers at Old Sturbridge Village, Massachusetts, but many people find such an accurate interpretation less exciting than an imaginary one.

Another variation on the Celtic fad is the discovery and reading of imaginary Ogam inscriptions. Ogam, a very simple alphabet, was the first writing system devised for use in Ireland, around the 4th century A.D. The idea of writing had been brought to Britain by the Romans in the first century A.D. The Ogam alphabet, however, was not based on the Roman one. It had no vowels and represented the consonants by patterns of simple vertical lines. These line patterns were similar to cracks that appear naturally in some types of rock. All across America, people found what looked like Ogam inscriptions. A few enthusiasts have "translated" some of the thousands of cracked rocks available, but this fad has essentially died out, at least for the time being.

Scratches on rocks are not always either natural in origin or deliberate fakes. Indians left marks on rocks across the continent that sometimes reveal important features of these people's religious beliefs. Indian petroglyphs (figures carved in stone) are often individually quite simple but crowded together on a large rock face in a very confusing way because the same rock surface is used by many artists over a long period of time. Unfortunately, the results are often so complicated as to be undecipherable.

Dighton Rock in Massachusetts may be the best example of this phenomenon. Pictures of the rock have been published in many books and articles, each time showing only the particular lines that each author wanted to emphasize. At the time of the Viking fad, the rock was believed to be a runestone. Since then it has been variously described as Phoenician (an ancient Mediterranean language), Chinese, Japanese, Portuguese, and even Mongolian script. Many Portuguese Americans live in the vicinity today, so Portuguese is the most popular current interpretation of Dighton Rock. There is a full-scale copy in Lisbon, but some of the markings on it have been removed so that the rock seems to bear a message in Portuguese. The harm in these imaginative interpretations is that

A stone with genuine Ogam inscriptions in a churchyard in county Kerry, Ireland. Ogam, a phonetic alphabet based on groups of parallel lines, was created in Ireland in the 4th century A.D. by someone familiar with the Roman alphabet. Naturally occurring marks on rocks in northeastern North America have been interpreted as Ogam inscriptions and held up as evidence of early explorations.

Archaeology in North America developed over the course of the 19th century and has become a highly skilled scientific profession in the 20th. This Iroquoian burial was professionally excavated in 1904 at the Ripley site in Chautauqua County in western New York by an expedition from the Peabody Museum, Harvard University, led by M. R. Harrington. Today professional archaeologists excavate burial sites only when absolutely necessary.

the legitimate significance of such inscriptions as records of prehistoric American Indians is not only ignored but often denied.

The same attitudes have distorted the study and understanding of unwritten Indian languages. The cultures and languages of American Indians are as rich and complex as any in the world. Yet included in the efforts to discredit American Indian cultures in the 19th century was the often repeated idea that Indian languages were simple, crude, and incapable of expressing complicated ideas.

People ignorant of other languages often assume that languages, especially "simple" ones, borrow words easily. But there is no such thing as a simple language, and few incorporate words of foreign origin as easily as English does. More than 200 languages were spoken north of Mexico before Europeans arrived on the continent. A few misguided authors compared selected vocabulary almost at random and cited certain supposed similarities to American Indian languages as evidence that hordes of Vikings, Celts, Egyptians, Phoenicians and other ancient Mediterranean people such as Libyans, Carthaginians, and Semites passed through the Americas. These transient visitors are supposed to have left behind a scattering of words in various Indian languages, like so many discarded artifacts. But these theories too are wrong, and the supposed relationships illusions. To suggest that the Zuni Indian language of the American Southwest derives from ancient Libyan, as one recent author has done, is at best foolish and at worst belittling to an ancient and honorable Indian nation—as well as being shoddy scholarship.

The examples of harmful myths in archaeology are too numerous to list in their entirety. Popular enthusiasm for American archaeology by people whose own roots go back to Europe, Africa, or Asia has often led to serious distortions of American Indian prehistory. Sometimes these have resulted from well-meaning ignorance of the evidence or of scientific methods. Often, however, pranks and frauds have contributed to the spread of false information.

In archaeology, unlike medical science, fraud and error do not endanger public health, nor, unlike slander and libel in newspapers, do they directly harm living people. Belief in popular myths may yield profits for careless or dishonest writers. But such belief is not the science of archaeology, and ultimately it exploits American Indians by distorting their pasts. The rest of us owe much more to the Indians, with whom we share the continent and the prehistory it still contains.

The American Indians' own myths and folklore can tell us much about their cultures and sometimes provide important clues for archaeologists. However, even here it is important to separate the truths that every culture conveys in its myths from the information that we can explore further through archaeological science.

The chapters that follow present the main themes of American Indian prehistory. It is a fascinating story that has been written in the ground over thousands of years. Its pages can be read and fully understood only through the science of archaeology. ▲

Excavation of an 11,000-year-old mammoth in southern Arizona by an Arizona State Museum team in 1952. In the background, University of Arizona paleontologist John Lance uncovers a lower jaw. Paleo-Indian stone projectile points were found among the bones.

THE
EARLIEST AMERICAN
INDIANS

There will probably always be disagreement over how long ago human beings first arrived in North America. There are a number of reasons for this ongoing disagreement. The earliest Indian immigrants were surely few in number, perhaps only a few small families whose food supply depended primarily on hunting. Their descendants on the American continents grew in number over thousands of years, from a few hundred to a few million. Thousands of archaeological sites are known, but it is not known how many are still undiscovered. Because populations were growing and moving into new regions all the time, it is certain that later periods produced more sites than earlier ones. Because there were so few of them, the earliest arrivals must have left only a few traces, and it can never be known for sure that what has been found so far includes some of those earliest traces. The evidence will never be more than scanty, and it will always leave much room for debate.

There is no disagreement, however, that the first people to enter the Americas were fully modern humans, *Homo sapiens* like ourselves. All of the skeletal remains of the earliest Americans ever found have been of physically modern humans. Modern human remains of earlier periods have been found in Europe, Africa, and Asia. None of the thousands of skeletal remains of premodern human ancestors have been found in the Americas; all come from Europe, Africa, and Asia. The logical conclusion is that humans evolved entirely in the Old World, and that the migration to the Americas occurred after they had become fully modern physically, sometime after about 40,000 years ago.

By about 40,000 years ago, stone tools had been made and used in Europe, Africa, and Asia for a very long time by earlier as well as modern humans. The Paleolithic (literally, old stone) ages are referred to in terms of the locations in the earth of the artifacts that help identify them. By 40,000 years ago in the Old World, tool industries had already passed through the stages commonly known as the Lower and Middle Paleolithic. Most later types of stone tools from Upper Paleolithic industries were produced by modern humans.

Throughout the Upper Paleolithic, people in Europe and Asia were gradually able to move farther north as new types of stone tools helped improve their hunting skills, housing, and clothing. By 35,000 to 30,000 years ago, some of these people were living near the edges of the ice sheets in northern Europe and at even more northerly sites in Siberia. American archaeologists could expect the earliest evidence of human life in the Americas to consist of fairly sophisticated tools left behind in the remains of equally sophisticated camps. There should be no fear that natural objects such as weathered pieces of stone might be confused with occasional crude tools found in isolation from other evidence of human habitation. People who could fashion only crude tools are not likely to have reached the Americas.

The habitable world of that time was very different from today's. Giant sheets of ice called glaciers covered all of what is now northern Europe and the northwestern parts of the Soviet Union. They also covered almost all of Canada and Greenland. Mountain glaciers capped the Alps, the Himalayas, the Andes, and the Rockies. The largest sheets were sometimes 3 kilometers (al-

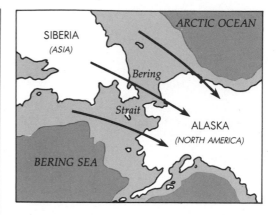

The Bering land bridge. Shaded area is 300 feet below present sea level.

most 2 miles) thick. Because so much water was frozen in the form of glacial ice, the world's sea levels were more than 80 meters (260 feet) lower than today. Many of what are today the islands of Japan, Indonesia, Malaysia, and the Philippines were part of the Asian continent.

More important, northeastern Siberia was linked to what is now Alaska by a land connection more than 1,000 kilometers (600 miles) wide. This land mass was so large and so different from the chain of small islands dotting the Bering Sea in that area today that scientists have given it its own name, "Beringia." Glacial ice was spotty in Siberia and Alaska, but the great North American ice sheet stretched from the Atlantic to the Pacific, completely isolating Beringia from the open lands to the south. Thus as the ancestors of the American Indians approached North America through northeastern Asia, they were able to move easily into Ber-

MEADOWCROFT ROCKSHELTER

Claims that dates of Paleo-Indian sites in North America are earlier than about 12,000 years ago have nearly always proven false. As of the late 1980s, the most carefully excavated and the most extensively dated early site on the continent has been the Meadowcroft site, south of Pittsburgh in western Pennsylvania. The site, a rock shelter or overhang, contained a deep deposit of earth and fallen rock before it was excavated. As archaeologists dug down they uncovered layers of evidence for every known period of human existence in the region, from recent centuries to Paleo-Indians.

Meadowcroft was excavated with unusual care. Razor blades were sometimes used in place of trowels, and the finds were put through nearly every chemical or physical test available to the investigators. Care was essential, for as the archaeologists dug through and below the level containing Paleo-Indian remains they entered a world of scientific controversy. It is widely accepted that people were in North America by at least 11,000 B.C., but there is no general agreement about earlier dates and suggestions that any finds date before then continue to arouse controversy.

In 1975 the Meadowcroft archaeologists published an article giving 17 radiocarbon dates for excavated material, and since then the number has grown to more than 50. Six of these dates are for material from the Paleo-Indian level at the site. The youngest dates to 10,850 B.C., an age acceptable to virtually all archaeologists. However, the oldest dates to 14,225 B.C., earlier than any generally accepted dating of Paleo-Indian material. For technical reasons, the laboratory had to specify an unusually large range of possible error for this date, so it could easily date a thousand years earlier. Nevertheless, when taken together, the six Paleo-Indian dates from Meadowcroft suggest that people were in southwestern Pennsylvania by at least 12,000 B.C., or 14,000 to 14,500 years ago. No technical reasons have yet been found that might indicate that the dates are in error. Just the same, archaeologists are waiting for independent confirmation of such early dates from additional sites.

There are objects that might be artifacts from still deeper levels at Meadowcroft. One of these is a fragment of material that appears to be basketry. But the two dates from these deeper levels both fall even earlier, before 17,000 B.C.. Few archaeologists are willing to accept these very early dates at this time. For such early dates to be accepted, there would need to be supporting dates of the same age from additional sites, as well as some finds in which the human origin of the artifacts is clearly demonstrated. Unique finds are always exciting, but good science requires reproducible results. In a historical science such as archaeology, reproducibility can only be achieved when similar finds occur at a number of sites.

The Old Crow site is on the Porcupine River in the northern Yukon Territory just over the border from Alaska. Artifacts found here were once dated to 25,000 and more years ago, but it is now thought that periodic flooding, erosion, and redeposition of soils led to incorrect dates. A key artifact excavated at Old Crow now appears to be only 1,400 years old.

ingia, only to be stopped from going farther by glacial ice. These first Americans probably had no idea that they had moved from one continent to another, and indeed, they actually had not. There would be no clear division between Asia and North America until the sea level was raised when the glaciers melted.

The Beringia connection is generally not disputed. Confirming evidence from the study of genetics and other physical characteristics makes it virtually certain that American Indians came from Asia. All of these pieces of biological evidence indicate that American Indians are more closely related to the people of northeastern Asia than to any other living human populations. There is an archaeological site in the northern Yukon Territory in Canada, just over the border from modern Alaska, that might contain some evidence about early Indians. Tools made by humans found at this site, called Old Crow, have been dated to 25,000 to 30,000 years ago. Over thousands of years, however, deposits at this river site have repeatedly eroded and been redeposited. As a result it is difficult to

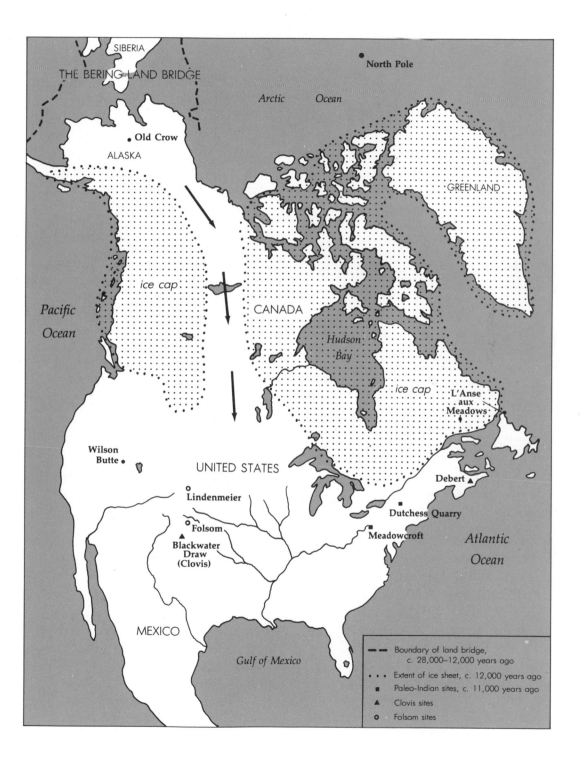

SIBERIA

THE BERING LAND BRIDGE

North Pole

Arctic Ocean

Old Crow

ALASKA

GREENLAND

ice cap

Pacific Ocean

CANADA

Hudson Bay

ice cap

L'Anse aux Meadows

Wilson Butte

UNITED STATES

Debert

Lindenmeier

Dutchess Quarry

Folsom

Meadowcroft

Atlantic Ocean

Blackwater Draw (Clovis)

MEXICO

Gulf of Mexico

- – – Boundary of land bridge,
  c. 28,000–12,000 years ago
- • • • Extent of ice sheet, c. 12,000 years ago
- ■ Paleo-Indian sites, c. 11,000 years ago
- ▲ Clovis sites
- ○ Folsom sites

RADIOCARBON DATING

The technique used to date archaeological remains by analysis of radioactive carbon was developed in 1946 by Willard Libby, who won the 1960 Nobel Prize in chemistry for this work. The element carbon is found in all living things, and a small proportion of that carbon is naturally radioactive. An element that is radioactive decays over a period of time. The small proportion of radioactive carbon in living, or organic, material is always the same, and its rate of decay is precisely known. Scientists use the term *half-life* to describe the amount of time required for half of a quantity of a radioactive element to decay. Radioactive carbon, known as carbon 14 or C-14, has a half-life of 5,730 years. This means that half of a given amount of carbon 14 will decay in 5,730 years. Thus, an amount of C-14 found today is half of the amount that would have been there 5,730 years ago; and that amount in turn would have been half of the C-14 of 5,730 years before that.

Libby reasoned that the age of any ancient object containing a measurable amount of carbon, such as charcoal or bone, could be found by determining the proportion of carbon 14 remaining in it. This method has been found to be highly reliable for determining dates within the last 50,000 years. This time span is quite long enough for archaeologists in the Americas, who find little material earlier than about 12,000 years old.

Since Libby's pioneering work, additional research has greatly improved the accuracy of radiocarbon dating. Radiocarbon dates have been compared with the precisely known dates of ancient tree rings. This comparison showed that the proportion of carbon 14 in the atmosphere has changed over time. It is also now known that the industrial revolution and nuclear weapons have drastically altered the balance of carbon 14 in the atmosphere. As a result, the technique is most accurate for objects that are more than a few centuries old. Further, some kinds of plants and animals absorb more of one form or isotope of carbon than of others. As a result, dates determined

determine accurately the dates of finds at various levels, and consequently there are disputes about the dates that have been suggested for key artifacts. One important artifact was at first dated to 27,000 years ago, but redating indicates that it may be only 1,400 years old.

If the Old Crow finds prove to be of a more recent time than previously thought, then the earliest Indians have still not been encountered by archaeological means in the far Northwest. The

by analyzing their remains are somewhat inaccurate and statistical adjustments must be made. Such dates may be either slightly too old or slightly too young depending upon the proportions of the different isotopes of carbon absorbed by a particular specimen.

Improvements have also been made in the equipment used to detect radioactivity. Modern particle accelerators, used to analyze the structure of the nucleus of an atom of an element, make it possible to obtain dates from much smaller samples. Still other technological improvements have reduced the margin of error in obtaining C-14 dates. As a result of all of these developments, radiocarbon dating is much more complicated and expensive but much more precise than it was only a few years ago.

Like all statistical techniques, radiocarbon dating has an inherent margin of error. This is expressed as plus or minus ($\pm$) a certain number of years from the date reported by the radiocarbon laboratory. A report might give the radiocarbon date of some pollen grains, for example, as 10,600 $\pm$ 150 years ago. This means that it is very likely, although not certain, that the actual date would be within the 300-year period of which the specified date is the middle (10,750 to 10,450 years ago). For statistical reasons there is still 1 chance in 3 that the actual date would be outside that range.

Other dating techniques are beginning to supplement radiocarbon dating in precision and at lower cost. Archaeomagnetism takes advantage of gradual changes in the location of the earth's north magnetic pole: Ancient hearths and some other archaeological features point to the north of their era, making it possible to date them against the known path of the pole's movement. Thermoluminescence is a dating technique based on the measurement of light radiated from ceramics when they are heated (particularly useful because small pieces of pottery are abundant at many prehistoric sites). The light emitted is proportional to the time that has passed since the pots were fired. But radiocarbon dating remains the mainstay of archaeological dating. All of these techniques are expensive, but their development has allowed archaeologists to be ever more certain about estimates of the ages of their finds.

earliest undisputed evidence from Beringia dates only to around 9000 B.P. (before the present). Surely something is still missing, because archaeologists are certain that many bands of hunters were scattered across North America south of the ice sheets in the period between 10,500 and 8000 B.P. These early Indian bands are usually referred to as "Paleo-Indians." They were probably descended from Asian immigrants who had been able to expand south-

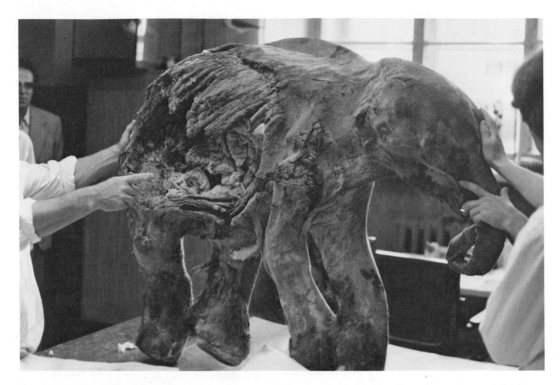

During the Ice Age, large game animals roamed through North America. Some crossed freely over the ice from Siberia, as did the first humans to enter the continent. This baby mammoth, which lived 10,000 years ago, was found frozen during an excavation in northeastern Siberia in 1977.

ward when the ice sheets began melting in about 14,000 B.P. This did not mean that the climate had suddenly become warmer. Glaciers move steadily, expanding outward from their centers of snow accumulation and melting steadily at their margins. By 14,000 B.P. the rate of melting at the ice margins was slightly ahead of the rate of expansion. However, the environment near the ice was still cold tundra: The earth below the surface was permanently frozen and only low plants, such as shrubs and mosses, could grow.

Ice Age North America might seem to have held little attraction for Paleo-Indians, but in fact it was full of large game animals, even near the edges of the glaciers. There were species of long-horned bison, horses, mammoths, mastodons, camels, tapirs, dire wolves, and giant ground sloths. Unlike the large game species of Africa and Asia, none of these species had evolved with developing human hunters as neighbors. For the American game animals, human hunters were new and dangerous predators. The animals probably lacked adequate defenses against skilled Paleo-Indian hunters armed with lethal weapons, such as stone-tipped spears. They certainly lacked the time necessary to acquire effective defenses by natural evolutionary means. The environmental changes at the end of the Pleistocene, or Ice Age, combined with the pressure of human hunters, pushed most of the large species to extinction. Musk oxen survived only in northern regions that no humans tried to penetrate until about 1,000 years ago. Most large animals simply died out as the species' death rates gradually exceeded their birth rates in the face of hunting pressure and environmental change.

The situation was just the reverse for the Paleo-Indians. The American landscape was wide open and full of game. Conditions became even better for the early bands of hunters as they moved southward. There was less need to hold down their own birth rates and little to prevent their rapid expansion across the land. Human biology and social needs set limits that influence the growth of human communities: There are limits to how many children a set of parents can have, limits to how many

Meadowcroft Rockshelter, in southwestern Pennsylvania, has yielded stone artifacts and charcoal that have been dated to 15,000 and more years ago. Each small white tag marks the location of a distinct soil level, pollen sample, or some other feature that has archaeological significance.

infants a woman can care for simultaneously, limits to how quickly those children can be raised to independence, and limits to how far away they will be willing to move when they grow up. However, we know from recent studies of living hunter-gatherers that, even within these limits, human populations can expand rapidly in both numbers and over space in a matter of only centuries. This might mean nothing more than a modest increase in the number of children raised by a couple, perhaps from an average of two to an average of three. Everything else being equal,

this seemingly small change in family size will rapidly lead to a significant population increase.

Thus it should probably not be a surprise that we have evidence showing that the Paleo-Indians were widespread in the Americas by 10,500 B.P. Paleo-Indian remains this old and perhaps a bit older have been found at a number of archaeological sites, including the Meadowcroft Rockshelter in Pennsylvania, Wilson Butte Cave in Idaho, and Dutchess Quarry Cave in New York. Some radiocarbon dates (see page 30) indicate that remains at the Monte

Dutchess Quarry Cave in New York State, where Paleo-Indian remains at least 10,000 years old have been excavated. By that time bands of Paleo-Indians were living throughout both of the American continents.

Verde site in Chile might be nearly that old. Many even older dates are claimed for several sites in both North and South America, but they remain controversial. It seems likely that Paleo-Indians had begun to establish themselves in the Americas at some time in the 3,500 years before 10,500 B.P.

After that date, the stone tools of the Paleo-Indians were characterized by distinctive and very carefully made projectile points. A projectile point is the stone tip attached to a hunting weapon such as a spear or arrow. Most are made of a type of stone referred to as chert or flint. The Paleo-Indian points are similar to the Upper Paleolithic points of Europe and Asia but also have special features that were probably invented in America.

The most widespread projectile point type is the Clovis point, so named because it was first identified in the 1930s at the Blackwater Draw site near Clovis, New Mexico. Archaeologists refer to the site that yielded the first or most typical example of a prehistoric culture as a *type site*. Blackwater Draw is the type site for the Paleo-Indian culture that produced Clovis points. The Clovis point was a spear point, sharp-edged and flat and made even flatter by the removal of long thin flakes of stone from both sides, leaving a "flute," or channel, on each face. Just how fluted points were made was a mystery until the technique was rediscovered in recent years. It is a difficult technique that calls for extremely precise removal of thin flakes from the piece of chert that

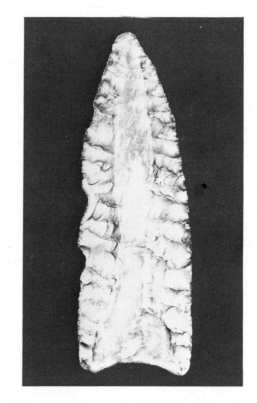

Paleo-Indian hunters secured stone tips to wooden shafts to form spears. Clovis points such as this one from a site in Nebraska were flat, sharp edged, and fluted (that is, a sliver of stone was removed from each face, or side, of the point).

serves as the base, or core, of the point. The flaking process proceeds upward from the base. To flake chert, the toolmaker either strikes the core piece with a round pebble hammerstone (percussion flaking), or presses a piece of bone or antler firmly against an edge of the core (pressure flaking). The flutes left when flakes were removed from the core helped to hold the point in the split end of a spear shaft.

Stone projectile point found at Folsom, New Mexico. Folsom points are fluted like Clovis points but are even more carefully fashioned, with fine tapered edges.

Fluting was not essential—later Indians got along for thousands of years with points that were fashioned without them. Clearly, Paleo-Indians put more effort into the production of fine points than was absolutely necessary. Furthermore, they chose raw materials for their beauty as well as for the ease with which they could be shaped and fluted. One point from Blackwater Draw was made from transparent rock crystal, beautiful but more difficult to work than standard chert.

Clovis and Clovis-like points are found all across the parts of North America that were south of glacial ice around 10,000–9000 B.P. but are more numerous in the East than in the West, where they were first found. They have been found as far northeast as the Debert site in Nova Scotia and as far south as Central America. They appear to have spread from the center of the continent northwestward into Alaska, back along the route first taken by immigrants from Asia. Clovis points have been found associated with the remains of mammoths, horses, forms of bison that are now extinct, and tapirs, a sure sign that Paleo-Indian hunters were at work.

Clovis points were replaced in the West by Folsom points. Folsom points associated with bison have been found only at the type site near Folsom, New Mexico, which was first excavated in 1927. The Lindenmeier site in Colorado has been better studied. Here Folsom points appear to date after 9000 B.P., by which time the focus of hunting had shifted away from mammoths and more toward bison as the Ice Age elephants became rare. Folsom points were also fluted and even more finely made than Clovis points. However, fluting was abandoned as the Pleistocene, big game, and the Paleo-Indian way of life all came to an end.

Variations in the locations of Paleo-Indian sites, their sizes, and the kinds of tools and features they contain tell us much about Paleo-Indian culture. Their tool kits included such objects as points, leaf-shaped knives, ovate knives, scrapers, gravers, spokeshaves, hammerstones, anvils, drills, awls, and pièces ésquillées. Pièces ésquillées are wedges that were apparently used to split antler and bone into workable slivers. Scrapers were used to scrape hide and plane bone and antler. Spokeshaves were apparently used to shape and smooth wooden shafts, probably spears and lances. Gravers were used to pierce hides and cut slots in bone or antler. Graver spurs, small sharp points for piercing or engraving, are sometimes found on scrapers, a combination tool that reminds one of modern combination gadgets. Taken as a complete kit, the range of tools indicates a technology focused on hunting, shaped or tailored clothing, and mobility. The Paleo-Indians traveled light, depended upon a lightweight set of well-made tools, and probably left heavy tools like hammerstones and anvils behind.

The fluted points lacked barbs, and their edges were usually deliberately dulled near the base, indicating that they were designed to be lashed securely to a shaft but not to become stuck in an animal. A spear might have been used over and over again by a hunter trying to bring down a large mammal—when it wounded the beast and fell away it could be retrieved by the hunter and thrown again.

The average size of the points indicates that they were attached to spears. American Indian hunters did not use the bow and arrow until thousands of years later. Like the Upper Paleolithic hunters of Asia, the Paleo-Indians apparently used spear-throw-

In 1927, chipped-stone projectile points were found in association with bison bones for the first time at a quarry in Folsom, New Mexico, evidence of Paleo-Indian hunting.

ers or *atlatls*, special sticks designed to serve as a virtual extension of a hunter's throwing arm. A spear hurled by an atlatl would have greater velocity than one thrown by the unaided arm. The typical spear-thrower would have been about a half meter (20 inches) long, with a handle at one end and a blunt hook at the other. The hunter held the spear-thrower at arm's length, with the hook inserted into a socket drilled in the butt end of his spear. He held the spear-thrower handle with three fingers in his palm, using his thumb and forefinger to steady the spear at its midpoint. On the attack, he would whip both spear-thrower and spear forward in an arcing motion, releasing his light grip on the spear and allowing it to be propelled by the end of the spear-thrower alone, which was by now moving with the speed of a tennis racket. With this simple device, a small spear had more speed, distance, and killing power than a larger spear thrown by hand.

Not only were fluted points skillfully made of exotic materials, but finished specimens are often found far from the places where they were quarried. Unlike other tools, which were usually made from common materials and used only by their makers, fluted points were made from materials not readily available and were apparently traded or given as gifts. Possible reasons for such exchanges are suggested by what is known about how scattered bands of more recent hunters lived. Such bands would often meet with each other for several purposes. A band was usually too small for young people to find marriage mates, and so they would have to look to neighboring bands instead. Hunters from several bands would find it advantageous to combine forces and form large hunting parties when the animals being hunted were particularly large or numerous. Related bands would also cooperate to share food in hard times. Thus there were many good reasons for members of different bands to build and maintain strong ties. Gift exchange would have been an important way to keep the ties of friendship and cooperation strong,

and the redistribution of fine fluted points is probably the best evidence of this kind of activity. A nice specimen might have traveled hundreds of miles as it passed from one proud owner to another. Each time the gift changed hands it would have created a new bond of friendship and obligation or strengthened an old one.

Paleo-Indian artifacts also tell archaeologists about the makeup of specific bands and the activities that went on within them. A small hilltop site containing only hunting tools would have been a camp from which the men could watch the movements of game animals. A small open site containing a full range of tools plus the remains of butchered game animals would have been a kill site used by a family band. A small site on a river's edge containing only food-preparation tools might have been the location where a team of women collected and prepared wild plant food. A large site with many hearths and a full range of tools would probably have been a favorite campsite repeatedly visited by one or more bands over the course of many years.

Examination of a variety of sites has allowed archaeologists to conclude many things about Paleo-Indian society. These people were highly mobile, and at first they wandered freely, expanding into many unoccupied regions. After the Paleo-Indians had occupied the most desirable regions of the continent, they remained mobile but gradually restricted their movements to specific territories.

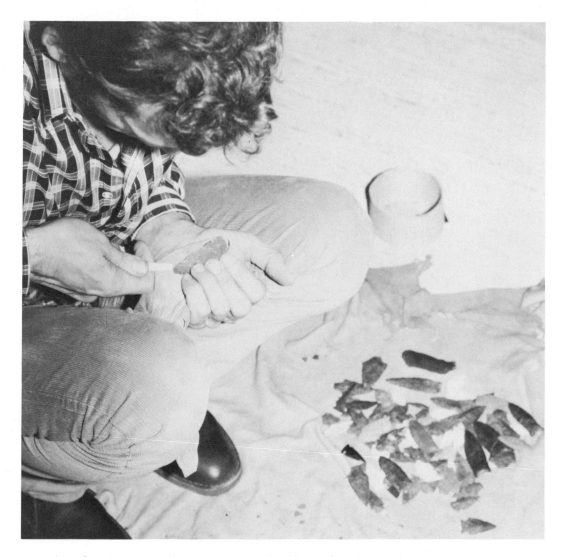

A modern flint-knapper replicates ancient toolmaking techniques.

Meanwhile, the environment was beginning to change as the great ice sheets melted away. The locations of plants and animals the Paleo-Indians used for food were not as predictable as they would be much later. Just the same, the Paleo-Indians were able to settle into seasonal migrations within their territories. These regular movements would have brought them together with neighboring bands from time to time, and gifts of points and food would be exchanged. Young couples would get married and most likely

A Siberian Ice Age house made of mammoth bones was reconstructed for a museum exhibit in the 1980s. Like their relatives who remained behind in northern Asia, Paleo-Indians made good use of every part of the animals they hunted.

join the band of the groom's parents. In hunting band societies, married couples from different groups usually end up living with the husband's, rather than with the wife's, family. This arrangement is known as patrilocal residence. (The reverse system, in which a newly married couple lives with the wife's family, is known as matrilocal residence.)

There can be no doubt that the Paleo-Indians were skilled hunters. From the tools that were apparently used to prepare and fasten animal hides, it can also be assumed that they wore well-tailored clothing. From the range of tools for hunting and preparing food, it can be assumed that they had detailed knowledge of how to gather and use small animals and plants for food. These people and their skills were new to the Americas. The ancient game animals that were here were already feeling the adverse pressures of a rapidly changing environment. The abilities of these strange new human hunters might have been the final blow. Even if Paleo-Indian attacks only reduced the animals' rate of reproduction, this extra pressure could have been enough to doom them. In any case, by 8000 B.P., the herds of the largest game animals were dwindling as rapidly as the great ice sheets. The landscape was changing fast, and the Paleo-Indians had to change too. The ways in which they changed 10,000 years ago would influence all future developments in prehistoric America.

The end of the Pleistocene and the extinction of large game animals brought an end to the Paleo-Indian way of life. Many of the same environmental changes occurred in Europe and Asia. The shift was not quite as dramatic in Africa, partly because there had never been huge glaciers there. Also, the big game animals of Africa had evolved for hundreds of thousands of years with human hunters evolving in their midst. Because these animal populations had been able to adapt over a long period of time to the rise of humans, the hunting capabilities of prehistoric peoples in Africa did not cause as great a reduction in their numbers.

The cold-loving mammoths and mastodons became extinct everywhere. Horses and camels became extinct in the Americas except for the cousins of the camel, the llama and its relatives, which survived in South America. Smaller bisons survived in North America, but the larger bison species became extinct. The critical difference between Eurasia and the Americas was in the set of medium-sized animals that survived in Eurasia but either died out or had never lived in the Americas. Everywhere, environmental changes at the end of the Pleistocene set the scene for the rise of human civilizations. The kinds of animals living on their continents would cause American Indian civilizations to be different from those of the Old World. The melting of glacial ice and the rise of sea levels cut the Americas off from the rest of the world, making certain that American Indians would be on their own in this development. Differences in opportunities and resources to work with made it certain that American civilization would be different, in spite of the similarities that human creators give to their civilizations everywhere. ▲

Spruce Tree House, a spectacular cliff-dwelling ruin in Mesa Verde National Park, Colorado.

THE
TRADITIONS
OF THE
SOUTHWEST

Archaeologists often discuss the evidence they find as being a reflection of prehistoric traditions. A tradition is a distinct way of life that continues for a substantial period of time. It may constitute an entire culture, or that part or phase of a culture that developed in a particular region or period. A tradition might last for thousands of years, extending over greater or lesser reaches of territory with the passage of time. As long as the evidence of a particular human way of life remains unchanged, archaeologists know they are dealing with the same tradition. When the cultural continuity is broken—that is, when new types of artifacts appear in the archaeological record—a new and different tradition has taken over.

Three major and several minor prehistoric cultural traditions have been identified and defined for the later prehistory of the Southwest. The Paleo-Indians were long since gone by the time these arose. The major traditions are known as Hohokam, Mogollon, and Anasazi. Some of the minor traditions, which developed near and sometimes between the major traditions, are Patayan, Sinagua, and Fremont. These major and minor traditions spread over most of what are now the states of Arizona, New Mexico, and Utah and sections of Colorado, California, and Nevada as well as the northern parts of the Mexican states of Sonora and Chihuahua.

The prehistoric traditions of the Southwest began to develop some time before 2,000 years ago. These traditions included the use of pottery and domesticated food plants such as maize (corn), beans, and squash. These crops had been domesticated centuries earlier in Mexico and spread northward from one community to another, or in some cases with migrating communities. Village life began in the Southwest by around A.D. 600. Many archaeologists have for a long time accepted the date of 3000 B.P. for the introduction of maize to the Southwest. However, this leaves a lag between the introduction of domesticated plants and the beginnings of

Basket with corn kernels.

settled village life. This has been difficult to explain because horticulture, the production of crops using small hand tools, is usually practiced only by settled communities. Recent reanalysis of radiocarbon dates indicates that maize may have been introduced as recently as A.D. 750. Because the revised dating brings the appearance of maize and the development of settled village life much closer together in time, the unexplained gap disappears.

Archaeological research can never be completed. Conclusions reached by archaeologists about almost any topic are subject to revision. There is still little certainty about Southwest prehistory prior to A.D. 600. However, the history

of the Hohokam following that time is fairly clear. Age estimates from some early sites have led investigators to conclude that the tradition was founded as early as A.D. 300. Other Hohokam sites seem to contradict this date and suggest a beginning date as late as A.D. 500.

Hohokam culture was located in the desert region of southern Arizona. This area is still the home of the Pima Alto and Papago Indians, who are widely believed to be the living descendants of the Hohokam tradition. It is probably very appropriate that the word *Hohokam* means "those who have gone" in the Pima language. It is possible that the people who originated this tradition traveled north into the Southwest from

Mexico, bringing Mexican traits with them. However, archaeologists generally assume that traditions develop in the place where their remains are found unless migration to that place can be clearly demonstrated. So far, for the Hohokam, it has not. Most archaeologists believe that the tradition developed in Arizona, influenced by trade and ceremonial interaction with the cultures in Mexico to the south.

Until recent years, archaeology in the Southwest concentrated on attempts to determine the chronology of sites and the cultures they represented. Archaeologists are now more concerned with studying cultural processes, the ways in which traditions develop, change, and give rise to new traditions. Archaeologists today are asking questions about how Hohokam came to develop in such a harsh environment and how and why the tradition changed over time. However, chronology is still important because cultural processes operate in a framework of time as well as space.

Archaeologists use artifacts as markers to help identify stages in the chronology of a tradition. Generations of archaeologists have used Hohokam pottery as one such marker. The people of this tradition made pottery from the tan-colored clay of the Arizona hills and decorated it with designs painted in darker orange-red clay. The Hohokam red-on-buff pottery vessels often have a shape that provides a large surface on which to display painted decorations. The details of these decorations are used to indicate periods within the Hohokam tradition. Examples of pottery that are similarly shaped and decorated are considered to date from the same period.

Other common objects of the Hohokam tradition include stone axes with deep grooves for attaching wooden handles. There are also flat stone slabs or palettes that might have been used to grind pigments, colored stones and earths. Some might have been used as mirrors when coated with a thin film of water. There are distinctive arrow points with deliberately jagged edges. Some elaborate shell ornaments have been found, most made of seashells from the Gulf of California. Some shells were cut into beads, pendants, or bracelets. Others were left whole and decorated with complex stone mosaics or etched by using weak acid solutions made from the juice of a cactus fruit. Little copper bells are also found in Hohokam sites and were probably imported from Mexico. These were made by the lost wax method in which a model of the desired final shape was made of wax. The wax was then encased in clay, leaving two or more openings. The metal was heated to the molten state and poured into one of the openings. As the hot metal entered the mold, it melted the wax, which escaped through the other opening. The metal took on the shape of the original wax model. After it cooled, the clay shell was broken open. The metal object was then finished, perhaps by filing to smooth rough edges, and polished.

When any of these Hohokam artifacts are found in a particular deposit, they serve as markers to date any accompanying objects or other evidence. Even more important, they give evidence of trade with Mexico or the Gulf of California coast, or of the existence of craft industries and cultural systems that operated for centuries in the Southwest. A cultural system is the way in which the various aspects, or cultural processes, of a people's way of life are organized. These cultural processes take form over time to allow populations to feed and reproduce themselves, and to give satisfaction and meaning to the lives of their individual members.

Structures found on Hohokam sites dating after A.D. 600 are similar to recreational and religious structures that are found in Mexico. Impressive ball courts have been uncovered in Arizona at the sites of both Snaketown and Pueblo Grande. Unlike the more elaborate ball courts found in Mexico, those of the Hohokam are large oval basins.

One of the two ball courts excavated at Snaketown in Arizona, a Hohokam site. The court is 100 by 130 feet and was constructed between A.D. 600 and 900. Balls made of rubber from Mexico were found at the site, but all we know about the game played by the prehistoric Southwestern people is that it probably had ceremonial significance.

Yet we can be fairly sure of their use because rubber balls obviously imported from Mexico were found associated with them. Snaketown is now being developed as Hohokam Pima National Monument, and Pueblo Grande is maintained as a museum and archaeological park by the city of Phoenix.

Archaeologists conclude that a site represents a chiefdom when that site is relatively large, contains structures for public use, and is surrounded by smaller communities of the same age. Such is the case at Mesa Grande, and other large centers where structures called temple mounds are found. These are low earthen platforms, usually only about 1 meter (3 feet) high and seldom more than 3 meters (10 feet) high. The temple mounds here and at similar sites in the American Southwest are small in comparison to the pyramids on which Mexican temples were erected. However, their presence suggests that these large central communities had control over the smaller communities nearby. Mesa Grande (which is now preserved as part of the Los Muertos complex in the city of Mesa, Arizona), was probably the center of a chiefdom, a political organization that incorporates two or more tribes or villages that would otherwise operate independently and has a permanent high-ranking governing structure.

A Hohokam community consisted of a cluster of shallow pit houses, or dwellings built into the ground. These were built of wattle and daub, a construction of walls made of poles and sticks and covered with mud. Each house was erected in a shallow depression dug down to the caliche, a pavementlike layer that lies just under the surface of much of the desert. The clusters of houses were built near complexes of irrigated fields.

We know that Hohokam farmers used irrigation to grow crops in the desert. This method of horticulture requires much more labor than either terracing or field contouring, which involve reshaping hill slopes to prevent soil loss through erosion, but it was extremely productive. The farmers tapped into rivers such as the Salt or the Gila upstream from where they wanted to plant their fields. To draw water off, they dug branching ditches away from the river. To get the water up to land above the river valleys where their fields were, Hohokam engineers sloped the ditches at narrower gradient angles than those of the rivers themselves. The Hohokam probably removed the earth by hand, using simple digging sticks and baskets, after it had been softened by the water. This system of branching ditches allowed them to direct the water farther and farther away from the river's main channel as it moved down the valley, into the nearly parallel ditches. A few kilometers from the river, the ditches ran along the edges of bluffs overlooking the flood plain of the river. Dusty fields on the flood plain were brought to life by irrigation water spilling from such ditches onto the fields below.

Irrigation enabled Hohokam farmers to produce two crops each year. One was harvested in March and April, after the snows had melted in the mountains, filling the rivers that fed the irrigation canals. The second was harvested in August, when summer rains fell in the mountains, filling the same rivers and canals.

The Hohokam cremated their dead, often placing the ashes in their distinctive red-on-buff pottery jars. Because archaeologists rarely find skeletal remains on Hohokam sites, we know little about the appearance of Hohokam people.

Crop failures and perhaps raiding by late prehistoric Apache immigrants from the north led to the political collapse of the Hohokam chiefdoms by A.D. 1450. By the time of the first Spanish exploration in the early 16th century, the chiefdoms were gone and the extensive irrigation systems they had created and maintained were abandoned. (Some of the abandoned ditches have been reopened within the last 100 years by modern immigrant farmers from the East.) The remnants of the Hohokam retreated to small scattered villages. Their probable descendants remain there today, still making a hostile desert bloom.

The Mogollon tradition occurred farther to the east, along the border between present-day Arizona and New Mexico. It began sometime in the 3rd century A.D., and later its settlements spread outward from this heartland. The distinctive marker for this tradition is its red-on-white pottery. Like the Hohokam, the Mogollon people lived in pit houses. As time went on, the communities contained more but smaller pit houses, suggesting that there was a shift in residential patterns. Perhaps Mogollon people went from living in large extended family groups to smaller nuclear families consisting of two parents and their children. The dates of sites in the Mimbres River valley in New Mexico indicate that the Mogollon people were expanding in numbers and in area through the 9th century.

The site of Casas Grandes in the present-day Mexican state of Chihuahua was within the expanded geographic range of the Mogollon tradition. Although the dating of the site is still controversial, major building probably began at Casas Grandes around 1060, declined after 1261, and ended by 1350. Through the course of nearly three centuries, the people of Casas Grandes gradually built a large village of individual rooms packed together in a community resembling a modern apartment complex. The location of the site, between the core of the American Southwest and central Mexico, has led some archaeologists to speculate that it was on a trade route for Aztec *pochtecah*, long-distance traders who also served as scouts for the expansion of the Aztec Empire in the 16th century.

Early Mogollon homes, built before 1000, were usually pit houses. After that date, the people increasingly built above ground structures clustered in

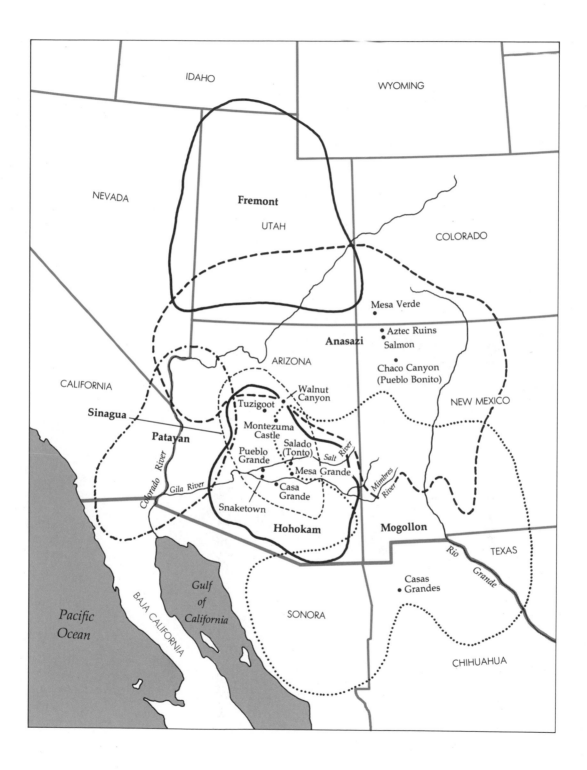

apartment complexes. This architectural style appears earliest at Mogollon sites in the north, and it seems likely to have been influenced by the culture that was flourishing at about that time in what is now northern Arizona and New Mexico, the Anasazi tradition. But the change in architecture may signal more than stylistic influences from another cultural tradition. The cultures in which apartment dwellings are customary, such as the historic Pueblo communities of the Southwest, follow matrilocal residence patterns, in which related women, along with their husbands and children, live in residential clusters of apartments within a larger house structure. Matrilocal residence is also common among village farmers in other regions. The emergence of apartment dwellings at Mogollon sites, then, may indicate that this system of residence after marriage was emerging in the Mogollon tradition through the years following A.D. 1000.

The appearance of ceremonial kivas around the same time supports the interpretation of a shift to matrilocal res-

Great Kiva, Chetro Ketl community, Chaco Canyon, New Mexico. These large underground spaces were probably the site of community rituals. Kivas, still used by Pueblo Indians today, are architectural holdovers from an earlier period when the people of the Southwest lived in pit houses.

Black-on-white Pinedale pottery, which was often used as a grave offering, is characteristic of the late Mogollon tradition.

idence pattern. Kivas are underground chambers built into the adobe apartment structures of the Southwest. They constitute a survival of pit house architecture and served as rooms in which related men, who did not live together in matrilocal communities, could meet and hold ceremonies. Some kivas, called "Great Kivas" because of their large size, measured as much as 10 meters (33 feet) in diameter. Only one of such size is found in a village, which suggests that Great Kivas served as ceremonial centers for entire communities. Smaller kivas found throughout the

apartment complexes apparently continued to serve the male members of particular clans. Each clan was a group of related individuals; in matrilineal clans, people related through the female line. Members of a particular clan believed that they descended from a common ancestor. Male clan members did not live together in this matrilocal society, so the kiva served as an important meeting place for them.

A distinctive black-on-white pottery style developed among the Mogollon in the Mimbres Valley of New Mexico during the same period. These vessels usually have geometric, human, and animal designs. They were often used as grave offerings and were ritually "killed" by being broken or punctured before being placed with the dead in graves. This pottery is very attractive to modern collectors, and the demand for it has led to looting and damage at many Mimbres sites, resulting in the loss of valuable archaeological information.

The Mogollon tradition began to decline around 1100. The territory covered by the tradition shrank rapidly, apparently collapsing in upon itself through the 14th century. This was also happening to other Southwest traditions around the same time. Warfare among

A detail of Anasazi pit-house construction exposed during excavation at Pueblo Bonito, in Chaco Canyon, New Mexico.

Mogollon people or with outsiders may have been one cause, and changes in the climate disrupted their system of food production. Some remnants of the Mogollon tradition might have moved in with Anasazi or Hohokam survivors. Zuni pueblo today is apparently at least in part made up of Mogollon descendants, but for the most part the tradition disappeared.

In the area where Arizona, New Mexico, Utah, and Colorado meet, now called the "four corners," villages of pit houses began to appear by 185 B.C. This was the start of the Anasazi tradition. *Anasazi* means "the ancient ones" in the Navajo language. At first the carriers of the Anasazi tradition did not manufacture pottery, and the early periods of the tradition, before A.D. 700, are known as "Basketmaker" from the predominant artifact type found at these sites. Later periods are characterized by pottery and houses more like those of the modern Pueblo Indians. They are consequently known as "Pueblo" periods. The first Pueblo period began around A.D. 700. All periods of the Anasazi tradition are well defined by tree-ring dates. Since early in the 20th century dendrochronology, or tree-ring dating, has been used to date southwestern sites very precisely, often to a particular year. The technique (see page 54) has been especially successful in determining the dates of Anasazi and some Mogollon sites, mainly because desert conditions make tree rings sensitive to widespread but minor variations in rainfall. The dry desert has also preserved wood well at many archaeological sites. However, local conditions at Hohokam sites have not preserved wood remains well, and archaeologists have to depend upon radiocarbon and other dating methods instead.

The earliest Anasazi pit houses were shallow and crude compared to later ones. Later pit houses were dug deeper, until what was once a smoke hole came to be the entrance to a house that was completely underground. The newer, deeper houses needed ventilation shafts to provide a draft to carry smoke out through the ceiling entrance. What had been the side entrance became the ventilation shaft in later houses. The Anasazi built small deflector walls in front of the shaft openings to regulate the draft. Many Anasazi sites from all periods are preserved in Mesa Verde National Park in southwestern Colorado. Visitors can see examples of the whole sequence of pit houses, which in later periods survived only as ceremonial kivas. They might notice a small hole in the floor between the deflector wall and the hearth pit. This is called a *sipapu*, and it symbolizes the hole through which the Anasazi believed humanity originally emerged from the underworld.

The Anasazi developed their own pottery styles after A.D. 700, borrowing many styles and techniques from the Mogollon and Hohokam. There were many black-on-white types. Around the same time, the Anasazi began to shift from pit houses to above ground apartments built of stone. They kept pit houses as ceremonial kivas, just as the Mogollon had done and for the same purposes. The Anasazi tradition also expanded its territory during this period. New villages appeared farther and farther from the original Anasazi core area, reaching their maximum extent in about A.D. 1100.

Between A.D. 700 and 950, most Mesa Verde villages were compact apartment complexes located on top of the mesa. But by 1150 almost all Mesa Verde villages had moved to more readily defensible shelters in the sides of the mesa's cliffs. Large natural rock overhangs provided enough space to construct towns such as Cliff Palace, which contains more than 200 rooms and 23 kivas. Access to the cliff dwellings was difficult and easily protected. The large proportion of kivas to rooms at Cliff Palace indicates that the town was probably a ceremonial center for many of the other smaller villages of Mesa Verde.

Another impressive series of Anasazi sites is found in Chaco Canyon National Monument, New Mexico. Chaco towns were connected to each other by a web of roads. Outlying sites such as Aztec Ruins near Aztec, New Mexico, and the Salmon site near Bloomfield, New Mexico, were also connected to the primary series of sites in Chaco Canyon by roads. We are still not sure just what the nature of the Chaco system was, but the archaeological evidence indicates that it eventually extended over 53,000 square kilometers (20,500 square miles) of what is now northwestern

(continued on page 56)

DENDROCHRONOLOGY

Dendrochronology is the determination of dates from the variations in thickness of the annual growth rings of a tree. Every year, a tree's trunk gets a little bigger, and the increase in size appears as a single dark circle around a cross section of the trunk after the tree has been cut down. As so often happens in science, a researcher came upon dendrochronology while searching for something else. At the beginning of the 20th century Andrew E. Douglass, an astronomer, was hoping to use variations in growth rings of trees in the American Southwest to understand cycles in the sun's output of energy. He found that the year-by-year variation in the thickness of tree rings was the same over the entire region, and that the varying thicknesses were due to regional fluctuations in the climate, particularly rainfall. The width of a growth ring is directly related to the amount of rainfall in a year; drought years produce narrow rings, and years when rainfall is ample produce broad rings. Douglass reasoned that, because each tree began forming tree rings at a different time, depending on its age, the pattern of annual variations in growth ring thickness in each individual tree would be unique. However, sections of a given tree's unique growth ring pattern would overlap sections of other trees that lived in the same period and region.

Douglass first worked with the cross section of a very old tree, a ponderosa pine, that had been cut down while it was still living. The outermost growth ring was laid down most recently, in the year when the tree was felled. By counting back to the center of the tree, Douglass had a tree-ring record going back for many years. This became the master log. He

Tree-ring patterns from successively older trees are matched to build a chronological sequence.

discovered that he could work back even further in time by matching the inner rings (representing the first years of the tree's existence) of a tree whose dates were known to the outer rings of slightly older timbers. That way he could continue to count back year by year beyond the oldest rings of the oldest living trees. He also extended his studies to the giant redwoods of California, which live 2,000 years and more. In this way, Douglass was able by 1919 to determine the cutting dates of redwoods back to about 1200 B.C., and by the end of the 1920s to determine the cutting dates of timbers in archaeological sites in the Southwest to the year A.D. 701. Ultimately the entire tree-ring sequence was diagramed, so that any wood found at an archaeological site in the Southwest could be compared with the charted pattern in order to determine where it fit in. In recent years scientists have used sections of ancient bristlecone pine trees to push the tree-ring sequence in North America back more than 8,000 years.

Despite the precision of dendrochronology, there are problems, as there are bound to be with any dating technique. Like skilled carpenters everywhere, prehistoric Indians often prepared or dressed timbers into final form by shaving off the outer rings. This makes it uncertain when the tree was cut, because there is no way to know how many outer rings have been removed. This can lead to age estimates that are too young. Furthermore, prehistoric people conserved resources and reused timbers from abandoned dwellings when they built new structures; such finds can lead to age estimates that are too old.

Tree-ring dating works best where environmental conditions were varied and generally stressful while the wood was growing, and where wood is best preserved. When there is great variation in climate, and especially in the amount of sunshine and rainfall, the variations in thickness of growth rings will also be great and distinctive patterns will show up clearly. The desert Southwest and the Arctic are both stressful environments for trees, and trees that survive there at all often show consistent variations in ring thicknesses throughout the region. Tree-ring dating does not work well in the Eastern Woodlands, where climate and rainfall are more similar from one year to the next. In this region, ring thicknesses vary more from locality to locality than from year to year. The thickness of a ring in a particlar tree might depend on whether it has been shaded by a larger tree nearby.

Wood preservation is good in the Southwest because the environment is dry and good in the Arctic because the frozen soil prevents decay. Wood can also be preserved in bogs or under water, where decay-causing oxygen cannot reach it. However, environments that foster this kind of preservation are the same environments that promote local variations in tree-ring thicknesses, so dendrochronology is seldom used to date wet wood samples.

(continued from page 53)

New Mexico. Large planned towns such as Pueblo Bonito were concentrated in Chaco Canyon but were also established elsewhere in the region. More than 125 sites in this network have been discovered, many linked by prehistoric roads. More than 400 kilometers (250 miles) of roads have been found and mapped so far. The most impressive towns in Chaco Canyon were large, D-shaped communities such as Pueblo Bonito, Chetro Ketl, Hungo Pavi, Una Vida, Pueblo del Arroyo, and Pueblo Alto, sites that are all open to tourists. Many of them contain Great Kivas which, like the Mogollon examples, were probably used for large community ceremonies.

Chaco towns were thriving places from 950 to 1300. Their locations, access roads, and artifacts all indicate that they were important centers in a widespread system of trade. Even as the boundaries of the Anasazi tradition shifted, the Chaco network held firm. Chaco Canyon was on the northern edge of Anasazi territory in the 10th and 11th centuries, but the territorial boundaries shifted so that Chaco was on the southern edge by the 12th century.

We still have much to discover about Chaco culture. Perhaps Chaco Canyon was both a ceremonial center and a center of trade, and both food and luxury goods, particularly turquoise, were traded. On the other hand, perhaps the Chaco system expanded primarily to provide space for a growing Chaco population. Outlying sites such as the Salmon and Aztec might have been

Handprints and other designs on a rock shelter wall at Canyon de Chelly, Arizona, a major Anasazi site.

either previously independent towns drawn into the system or colonies established by it. The road network might have been designed to carry luxury items, food, or both. Part of the excitement of southwestern archaeology comes from the many questions that are still waiting to be researched and answered.

(Many Anasazi sites in Chaco Canyon and elsewhere are open to the public. State road maps mark many that are protected by government agencies and kept open for tourism. At Canyon de Chelly National Monument, for instance, visitors can walk or ride official tour trucks to several ruins.)

Beginning around A.D. 1300, the territories of the Anasazi and all the other Southwest traditions shrank drastically. Sites on the fringes of the territories were abandoned first, followed by those closer to the traditions' centers. The total population also declined, and within a century each tradition was reduced to a few core communities. The abandonment of the Southwest has for decades been attributed to a disastrous drought that is recorded in tree rings for the years 1276–99. But this explanation is no longer universally accepted. Whatever caused the Anasazi retrenchment, we do know that it was followed by invasion. But there is little strong evidence of the Navajo and Apache invaders until around 1500. Instead of being a cause of the abandonment of farming villages across the Southwest, the arrival of the invaders could have been an effect of it. Within

decades the Navajo and Apache were joined by the Spaniards, and the Indian villages of the Southwest came under both native and foreign domination by the early 17th century. But even after several hundred years of occupation and struggle, the descendants of the major Southwest traditions persist today as vigorous communities.

Fremont was a minor tradition that developed in what is now Utah, where small villages similar to those of the Anasazi have been excavated. This development might have begun as early as A.D. 400, but whether it came about when some Anasazi people migrated into Utah or was created by local Indians under Anasazi influence is still being debated. Fremont sites began to be abandoned as early as 950. The tradition was contracting by 1150, and only a few villages survived after 1300. It is still uncertain which, if any, of the historic Indians of the western deserts are descendants of Fremont. Fremont culture could have belonged to ancestors of modern groups such as the Shoshone. Until that question is answerd, the fate of the Fremont people will be unknown.

The Patayan tradition, sometimes called Hakataya, is considered another minor tradition in Southwest prehistory. Its earliest pottery dates to around A.D. 500, but the Patayan people never developed the large villages that mark the major Southwest traditions. The tradition appears to have been carried by Yuman Indians of the Colorado River region. Modern descendants still live in western Arizona and southeastern California. The best known of these peoples are probably the Havasupai, who live in a beautiful, remote part of the Grand Canyon.

Several regional variants related to Patayan have been defined. One of them developed into Sinagua culture in the Verde Valley of central Arizona. This location was between the Hohokam territory to the south and the Anasazi to the north. The Sinagua people developed a hybrid culture that drew upon the major traditions around them. Their culture flourished after 1100, mainly as a result of the eruption of a volcano. The eruption at Sunset Crater deposited a natural ash mulch in the Verde Valley. This mulch so enriched the soil that Sinagua farmers were able to produce bumper crops for 200 years. Tuzigoot and Montezuma Castle are fine examples of Sinagua stone architecture built during this time. Both are national monuments. "Montezuma Castle" is an unfortunate name, for it is not a castle and had no more to do with the Aztec ruler Montezuma than Aztec Ruins, New Mexico, had to do with his empire. Both were named by 19th-century explorers who let romantic enthusiasm get the better of historical accuracy. Walnut Canyon National Monument, near Flagstaff, Arizona, is a collection of dozens of Sinagua cliff dwellings.

When the effects of the volcanic ash wore off and normal soil conditions returned, the Sinagua people found themselves badly overextended. The Verde Valley area could no longer support the enlarged Sinagua population, and it was generally abandoned after 1300. Sinagua groups left their valley to join or live near villagers of other southwestern traditions. Tonto National Monument, near Roosevelt, Arizona, is a cliff dwelling built by some of these refugees. Others moved to Hohokam territory, where they formed joint communities with their Hohokam hosts. The migrants' culture is called Salado when it appears in Hohokam territory. The site of Casa Grande, Arizona (not to be confused with the Mexican site of Casas Grandes), provides an example of this process. While Hohokam people continued to cremate their dead and bury the ashes in traditional red-on-buff vessels, the Salado immigrants made red, black, and white polychrome (multicolored) vessels for burial with uncremated remains.

After 1300, the Salado/Hohokam communities built large rectangular adobe villages. The adobe outer walls of these villages enclosed plazas containing huge mud-brick structures. This was a major departure from traditional Hohokam architecture, which consisted of smaller structures. The villagers constructed the Great House at Casa Grande by laying down layer after layer of adobe mud bricks. The walls were made thick and massive at their bases but tapered towards their tops. The Great House was four stories high at its central core, although at ground level the central room was unusable, filled in with solid adobe to add

Montezuma's Castle is a well-preserved Sinagua-tradition cliff dwelling. Named by a 19th-century explorer with an overactive imagination, it actually has nothing to do with Montezuma and is not a castle.

strength at the base of the structure. It can be guessed that the Salado immigrants had been accustomed to working with stone masonry, such as that seen at Tuzigoot and Montezuma Castle, but were now forced to use adobe because Hohokam country lacked good stone for house construction. The Salado may have used adobe walls of such great thickness because they mistrusted this new, seemingly unsturdy, building material. Like so many other southwestern sites, Casa Grande is a national monument, near Coolidge, Arizona. It also contains a ball court such as those in Snaketown and Pueblo Grande described earlier.

Because of the extent of architectural remains and the richness of the artifacts found within them, southwestern sites have long been a focus of archaeological interest. Furthermore, tree-ring dating has allowed more precise dating in this region than in other parts of North America. For all of these reasons, much is already known about the prehistory of the Southwest, and much more is certain to be discovered in the future.▲

Adena burial mound, Miamisburg, Ohio.

THE
NATIONS
OF THE
EASTERN WOODLANDS

The end of the Ice Age led to many changes in the landscape of North America. Glaciers melted away, leaving behind clay, sand, and gravel that gradually turned into soil. Trees and other plants flourished once more, forming young forests, and the animals that depended upon them flourished as well. It took many centuries for the soils and forests to develop. Pollen grains from many thousands of years ago have been preserved in bogs, leaving a record of this slow process and of the changes in climate from Ice Age patterns to those we know today. The forest evolved to keep up with the gradually changing climate.

The small, scattered bands of Paleo-Indians that spread across North America at the end of the Ice Age confronted new environments that forced them to make changes in their way of life. The big game animals they had hunted were disappearing. The open tundra of the Ice Age was giving way to closed-in forests. Even in southern regions of North America where there had been no ice sheets the environment was changing in ways that made the old Paleo-Indian way of life impossible.

The region known to archaeologists as the Eastern Woodlands gradually took on its modern characteristics. Today, vast forests stretch from the Great Lakes southward to the Gulf of Mexico and from the Mississippi River eastward to the Atlantic. There is much environmental variation within this large region, but few geographic barriers to hinder population movements. In southern Florida the forest environment becomes subtropical, but elsewhere the Eastern Woodlands is predominantly temperate forest. To the north and at higher altitudes elsewhere maple and beech trees dominate, giving way to spruce, pine, and fir on the northern fringes and higher peaks. The southern woodlands contain more oak, chestnut, and tulip trees, which give way to pines on the sandy coastal plains.

The woodlands environments were more productive than the Ice Age tundra, containing more plants and animals, in greater variety. The descendants of the Paleo-Indians found that they could subsist in smaller territories. Because the modern woodlands were stable over long periods, the Indians were now able to schedule their movements between a variety of predictable food sources. They could plan on returning every year to favorite locations within their territories to hunt the same game as they had the previous year at that season or to gather the same nuts, berries, and roots. Perhaps they would net fish at a favorite stream every spring, gather strawberries and other fruits in a favorite meadow every summer, hunt deer in a certain forest every fall. Through trial and error the Indians learned how to make the most effective use of their environment.

The more abundant and predictable food supply supported a larger population and specialized occupations. As the human populations grew, regional cultures became increasingly self-sufficient. The far-reaching interdependence of earlier Paleo-Indian bands gradually came to an end. The new regional cultures, with their increased population densities, had little need for long-distance contacts.

The periods following the passing of Paleo-Indians are called Archaic. Archaeologists often refer to Early, Middle, or Late Archaic period, or to specific types of Archaic culture with identifying names such as Maritime Archaic. A period or culture may be called a "tradition" when it is of long duration. The various Archaic cultures lasted from around 8000 B.C. to around 1000 B.C. in the Eastern Woodlands. The Early Archaic lasted from 8000 to 6000 B.C. The Middle Archaic followed until around 4000 B.C., and the Late Archaic followed this for the 3000 years leading up to 1000 B.C. These dates are approx-

This birdstone of banded slate was used as a weight to give added power to a spear-thrower. The spear-thrower itself added force for hurling a stone-tipped weapon.

A curved blade of copper, cold-hammered 3,000 years ago by northern Woodland people who lived in the upper Great Lakes area. Their distinctive way of working chunks of metal ore has given them the name of Old Copper *culture.*

imate. There were numerous variations over both time and space, but archaeologists have detected distinct cultural traditions marked by the changing tools and food remains found in Archaic sites throughout this time period. By the Late Archaic there was a great variety of tool styles and ways of life in the region.

The great variety of languages spoken by the people living in the Eastern Woodlands by A.D. 1500 most likely had its beginnings in the Archaic periods. There were at least five language families, including dozens of languages in the Eastern Woodlands, by the time Europeans arrived in North America. Some languages became extinct so early that we are not sure which families they belonged to, but most of the known languages belonged to the Algonquian, Iroquoian, Caddoan, Siouan, or Muskogean families. Perhaps all of these derive from a small number of Paleo-Indian languages. Some linguists are convinced that Siouan, Caddoan, and Iroquoian languages all developed

from a common source; others have tied Algonquian and Muskogean to another common source. The gradual subdivision of cultures and of the few languages that eventually developed into language families must have begun in the Early Archaic.

The population center for the people speaking the Algonquian languages seems to have been the basin of the Great Lakes. The speakers of one or more of these languages appear to have spread northward from the basin across what is now eastern Canada. In later times the speakers of the branch of languages known as Eastern Algonquian spread southward along the Atlantic coast.

The Iroquoian-speaking people may originally have lived in the Appalachian Mountain region, later spreading northward into the lower Great Lakes basin. Those who spoke Siouan and Caddoan languages may have had their early development in the western part of the Eastern Woodlands, through which run the Mississippi River and its vast network of tributaries. The histories of both these language families are complicated by their speakers' rapid spread westward onto the Plains after A.D. 1500. Muskogean languages have their homeland in the American Southeast.

Archaic developments in the Eastern Woodlands are marked by careful use of regional food resources. Because each region had its own expanding and increasingly self-sufficient population, trade and exchange tended to go on within regions but not between them. The long-distance exchange of beautiful spear points between Paleo-Indian bands disappeared in the earliest Archaic period. In general, the emerging independent cultural regions tended to be defined by river basins. The interaction of people was easiest within these natural territories, but more difficult across the hills and mountains that separated them. All of these tendencies meant that there was increasing cultural diversity over the Eastern Woodlands.

Archaic cultures were inventive within their specialized regions. Where oak forests predominated, Indians learned to harvest acorns, process the acid out of them, and convert them into a nutritious flour. Where fish filled rivers, Indians invented traps, netting, weirs (fences built into streams to trap the fish), and smoking equipment to catch and preserve them. They found uses for plants we regard as weeds, such as sunflower, goosefoot, pigweed, knotweed, maygrass, and marsh elder. Gradually plant gatherers learned to encourage the natural growth, and over

(continued on page 73)

An animal that may be a bear cub decorates a shell gorget, an ornament worn on a band around the neck. About 23 centimeters (9 inches) long, it was engraved about 3,000 years ago by people who lived in the Great Lakes area.

FROM AND OF THE EARTH

The artifacts that archaeologists have found in North America speak to us about the lives of American Indians in prehistoric time. Much of what archaeologists find in the earth is made from the earth—pottery made of clay, tools and adornments made of stone or metal. Using the materials provided by their natural environment, people in every part of the continent made the objects they needed for cooking, clothing, shelter—the necessities of life. But human beings are inventive creatures, and they like to adorn themselves as well as the objects they use; often, they lavished such care on decorating these practical objects that today, hundreds of years later, we still appreciate their beauty. Archaeologists are not always certain of the use or significance of every object they find. The materials used, however, and the techniques with which the ancient people made these objects provide additional information about a way of life that developed in North America over thousands of years.

Mogollon tradition bowl and jar, black and white paint on red clay. Women were traditionally the potters among the American Indians.

Mimbres bowl with parrot design from Hawikuh, whose people may have been ancestors of the Zuni Pueblo people. Hawikuh is in New Mexico, a few miles from Zuni, near the Arizona border.

Mimbres bowls. The Mogollon people living in the Mimbres valley of New Mexico were superb potters.

A classic black-on-white Mimbres bowl. Bats often appear on Mimbres pottery.

A Mogollon jar. Indian women did not have pottery wheels and shaped their pots by hand.

Hohokam jars, in the style archaeologists call Sacaton red-on-buff. The Hohokam people cremated their dead and interred the ashes in pottery jars with inverted bowls for covers.

Anasazi bowl. Several Anasazi pueblos, some containing hundreds of rooms, fill Chaco Canyon in northern New Mexico.

Hohokam pottery in a variety of shapes. Pottery of this tradition is characterized by strong patterns and dramatic forms. The pottery forms often present broad surfaces for decoration, usually geometric.

Embossed copper portrait with such typical
Southern Cult features as an ear spool and
forked eye design.

Figures of a kneeling woman and man, about two feet tall, carved from solid blocks of marble. They were found with the remains of four burials in a mound in Etowah, Georgia, a large community that is one of the best-known sites of the late Mississippian Southern Cult tradition.

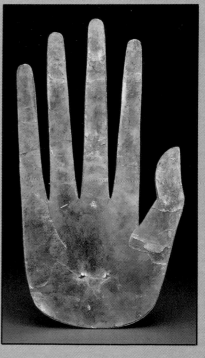

Hand, cut from mica, 28 centimeters (10 inches) long, from a Hopewell site in Ohio.

This stone beaver is a Hopewell platform pipe bowl; there is a hole in his back for tobacco.

This wooden figure from Key Marco off the Florida coast may represent a cougar deity or a human wearing a cat disguise.

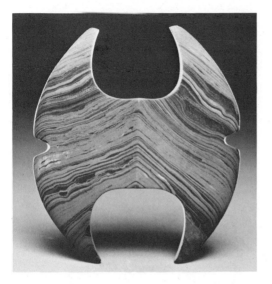

Carved stone weight for an atlatl or spear-thrower. The use of stone weights to give their spear-throwers extra power was a major technological advance of the Archaic people of the Woodlands.

(continued from page 64)

many years beds of such plants produced more seeds or tubers than they would have without human encouragement and regular harvesting. The Indians learned to make the environment more productive by burning off undesirable vegetation to encourage food plants and create meadows for herds of deer.

The bow and arrow were not yet Indian weapons, and were probably not used in the Woodlands until after 1000 B.C. The spear-thrower, which had been used by the Paleo-Indians, was still the principal weapon. It worked well, as it had for thousands of years, but Archaic Indians added a new twist. Archaeologists have found evidence that stone weights were tied to the wooden shafts of spear-throwers. Some of the stone weights have holes drilled through them so that they could be slipped over the spear-thrower shafts. Experiments by archaeologists using modern reproductions have shown that there is only an advantage to weighting the spear-thrower, by whichever method, if its shaft is also made of flexible material. In fact, the holes drilled in the weights are quite narrow, a sign that the spear-thrower shafts were so thin that any nonflexible material of that size available at the time would have snapped on the first throw. Therefore Archaic hunters must have discovered the advantage of flexible shafts that golfers and fishermen depend on today. If Paleo-Indian hunters could whip their rigid spear-throwers with the speed of a tennis racket, Archaic hunters could snap their flexible spear-throwers with even greater force. More than 2,000 years later, in ancient Mexico, where heavy spears were required to pierce an enemy's thick armor, the spear-thrower was still in use. In America north of Mexico, where hunting was more important than conquest, and warriors valued mobility more than armor, the bow and arrow would become the favored weapon.

The encouragement of a few native plants gradually became actual cultivation. As early as 2500 B.C., some Archaic cultures were cultivating gourds and squash, plants that most likely came to them from Mexico. These early cultivated plants probably kept hunters and gatherers from starvation in years when nature failed to provide enough food. Production and storage of surplus food is good insurance, and it is something that most modern people take for granted. Hunters and gatherers, however, also depended upon sharing as a means to survive periods of food shortage. In hunting and gathering communities, people who store food are regarded as selfish if they refuse to share it. People will not be motivated to overproduce and store food for future use if social pressure is likely to force them to give it away when a neighbor faces a shortage. Thus we can be sure that some social changes developed when people began to produce and store food surpluses. Food preservation and storage must have become group activities. As bands joined one another in order to centralize and protect their investment in surplus food, local groups would have taken on a tribal character. A tribe is by definition two or more local bands bound together socially and politically that act in their own interests and exclude other bands and tribes from that activity. As this cooperative behavior led to larger and larger social groupings, some leadership structure must have developed. In small groups everyone knows everyone else, and decisions can be made informally by cooperating individuals. Groups of more than about 500, however, require formal leaders to cooperate effectively, largely because human beings cannot manage that many individual relationships. Larger groups re-

quire ranking, leadership, delegation of power, and even social classes if they are to operate as a whole. The Archaic ended in the Eastern Woodlands not only with the development of cultivation and the production of food surpluses, but also with the development of formal leadership and social inequities. Archaeologists see evidence for social inequities primarily in finds that show elaborate burial rituals in which some individuals clearly received special treatment. These burial mounds are the most important markers of the new Woodlands cultures.

Archaeologists first uncovered burial mounds in the Eastern Woodlands more than 100 years ago. Unfortunately, advanced archaeological techniques were not generally available at the time, and many burial mounds were excavated by looters rather than by professional archaeologists. Looting, although still a serious problem, is less common today. But many of the mounds holding important archaeological information were ruined before that information could be gathered through systematic investigation. Despite the loss of much of the evidence, enough remains for archaeologists to detect the rise of Woodland cultures after 1000 B.C. At many sites, pottery has been found alongside other artifacts. Pottery making also appears to have come into the Eastern Woodlands from Mexico, probably spreading from one local culture to another along the coast of the Gulf of Mexico. It was first established in the southern part of the Eastern Woodlands, spreading throughout the region from there.

Perhaps the best known Early Woodland culture is Adena, which began in what is now Ohio by around 700 B.C. More than 200 Adena sites have been found in southern Ohio and portions of West Virginia, Pennsylvania, Kentucky, and Indiana. Adena Indians built many burial mounds by piling up quantities of earth. The largest of these is 21 meters (68 feet) high, still standing near Miamisburg, Ohio.

Such earthworks were constructed on numerous Adena sites. The Adena Indians put up ridges of earth in large circles, squares or pentagons or along the edges of natural hills. Many of these are up to 100 meters (330 feet) in diameter, but they seem to have been built as sacred enclosures rather than as fortifications. Sometimes the earthworks have interior ditches, which looked like moats to some early archaeologists. But the enclosures contain burial mounds, not castles.

For burial within these mounds, bodies were sometimes put in simple clay-lined basins, at other times in log tombs big enough to hold as many as three bodies. Often, the dead were cremated before being placed in even simpler graves. The dead in the more elaborate graves were frequently smeared with red ocher or graphite and provided with more high-quality goods for the deceased to take with them on their journey. Some smaller mounds were built all at once for a single individual; others were left open as mausoleums so that new burials could be added. These varying types of graves make it clear that some people had much higher status than others and that they were given far more elaborate burials in recognition of their position.

Adena potters at this period made crude pottery that played no important role in burial rites. Adena graves often contain other objects, however, such as reel-shaped gorgets (ornaments worn at the neck), small hand-sized stone tablets, and tubular pipes of banded slate or some other fine-grained stone. The tablets often had carved designs, either curved lines or abstract animal shapes. Birds of prey were especially popular. We are not sure what the function of these tablets was, but they might

Adena people, who lived in the vicinity of what is now southern Ohio, buried an assortment of precious objects with their dead. Tablets such as this, carved of stone, may have been coated with pigment and used to stamp designs on the body or on cloth.

have been used as stamps for fabrics or body painting and tattooing.

The tubular pipes indicate that tobacco was being smoked, but archaeologists have not yet found the tiny seeds of the tobacco plant in any Adena sites. Smoking originated in South America and spread northward, and the existence of Adena pipes tells us that tobacco smoking and the complex ritual that went with it were already present in North America by this time. In North America, tobacco smoking was consistently linked with the beliefs and practices associated with shamanism. Shamans were people (usually men) believed to possess supernatural powers. The Adena Indians believed that these men had the power to leave their bodies, often in animal form, when under the influence of strong tobacco or some other drug. Shamans were sometimes curers, typically treating disease by "sucking" its cause out of the body of a sick person. Tobacco was also smoked socially, and when Europeans arrived it was often an important part of meetings and negotiations between them and the Indians. The appearance of tobacco pipes in Adena culture signals much more than the simple controversial personal practice that smoking has become in modern times.

Long-distance trade was revived in Adena times, after having almost disappeared during the Archaic. But it was now more complex than the casual hand-to-hand trade that had characterized the Paleo-Indian period. Adena

traders imported raw materials from various places in the Eastern Woodlands, turning them into finished luxury goods that were eventually placed in the more elaborate burials as grave goods. Paleo-Indians had exchanged only practical items in finished form, and the production of luxury grave goods was not part of their culture. Adena artisans acquired chunks of native copper in trade from northern Michigan. They hammered the copper into bracelets, beads, rings, gorge[and axes. Adena society was probab[still structured around family and cl[membership. The practice of long-di[tance trade and the unequal treatme[of the dead, however, suggests th[high-ranking clan chiefs were probabl[in charge of conducting trade. In som[American Indian cultures known fror[historic times, clan heads fulfilled this kind of role and held a similar social position.

The center of Adena culture was in Ohio, but there are traces of it in many other places in the Eastern Woodlands. Adena goods can be found at sites as far away as Vermont, eastern New York, New Jersey, and Maryland. Archaeologists once thought that such outlying sites were locations of Adena bands that had migrated out of Ohio. However, it now appears more likely that the Algonquian- and Iroquoian-speaking people in these areas supplied raw materials to Adena craftsmen, and that a few finished objects found their way back to these hinterlands in exchange.

ADENA-HOPEWELL SITES AND RESOURCES

ONTARIO

QUEBEC

MAINE

St. Lawrence River

L. Superior

copper

silver

MICHIGAN

L. Huron

VERMONT

NEW HAMPSHIRE

MINNESOTA

L. Michigan

L. Ontario

Point Peninsula

NEW YORK

MASSACHUSETTS

CONNECTICUT

RHODE ISLAND

WISCONSIN

Effigy Mound

L. Erie

PENNSYLVANIA

NEW JERSEY

galena (lead)

IOWA

River

Mountains

MARYLAND

DELAWARE

INDIANA

OHIO

chert

Newark

Miamisburg

Mound City

Missouri

ILLINOIS

Fort Ancient

WEST VIRGINIA

Appalachian

VIRGINIA

Chesapeake Bay

River

chert

chert

Serpent Mound

River

Ohio

KENTUCKY

mica
crystal
chlorite

MISSOURI

Mississippi

NORTH CAROLINA

TENNESSEE

River

Tennessee River

SOUTH CAROLINA

ARKANSAS

GEORGIA

Atlantic

Ocean

LOUISIANA

ALABAMA

MISSISSIPPI

pottery

shark
barracuda
turtle shell

FLORIDA

whelk
alligator
tulip shell
olive shell

Gulf of Mexico

· · · · · Extent of burial mound construction,
          700 B.C.–A.D. 1000

– – – Extent of Hopewellian complexes

▨ Adena-Hopewell heartland

Mound City, near Chillicothe, Ohio, consists of a rectangular earthwork enclosing a field of Hopewell burial mounds. The site is maintained as a national monument.

Adena culture reached its peak in Ohio by 100 B.C. and disappeared there by A.D. 400, but it may have lasted until A.D. 700 in West Virginia. Adena was replaced in Ohio by Hopewell culture. Hopewell artisans, using Adena ideas as a basis, elaborated upon them to produce even larger and more complex grave goods. Like the Adena people, the Hopewell (who might have been their direct descendants) built elaborate burial mounds. A typical mound might be 12 meters (40 feet) high and 30 meters (100 feet) across at the base. Like the Adena, the Hopewell often built large earthworks around their burial mounds, but these were much more elaborate than any ever attempted by Adena architects. The Hopewell earth-works are circular, rectangular, square, and octagonal, sometimes more than 500 meters (1600 feet) in diameter. Two or more of them are sometimes connected by broad causeways. At Mound City, Ohio, a large square earthwork encloses a field of burial mounds. At Newark, Ohio, a complex series of huge geometric earthworks now contain a golf course but originally enclosed several burial mounds. The great Serpent Mound in Ohio, which may be either Adena or Hopewell, appears to have been a sacred effigy and not a burial place.

Hopewell grave goods were also more elaborate than Adena ones. The Hopewell people hammered large copper nuggets into the shapes of functional tools such as axes, adzes, celts (chisellike implements), and awls. Other pieces were beaten into spool-shaped ear ornaments, cut-outs, gorgets, beads, pendants, panpipes, and even artificial noses. The flat cut-outs are shaped like snakes, hands, heads, bird talons, and other forms, and seem to have been made only to be placed in graves. Copper sheets were embossed with designs, and at least the heavy ones were used as breastplates. One well-known copper piece is a headdress shaped like a pair of deer antlers. The Hopewell people also hammered iron nuggets of meteoric origin, as well as gold and silver, into thin sheets of foil, which in turn were used to cover ear spools, adzes, and other objects made of such less valuable materials as bone and antler.

The Hopewell people also valued exotic minerals, shells, and animal teeth. They kept crystals of galena, quartz, and chlorite as charms. They imported mica, a translucent mineral that forms in sheets, from the Appalachian Mountains to make cut-outs in the same shapes as the copper ones. The Hopewell people chipped stone tools from colorful stones such as cherts, chalcedony (a high grade of chert), and obsidian (dark volcanic glass). Some of the cherts were available in Ohio, but the obsidian came from what is now Yellowstone Park. Conch, turtle, and other shells, and the jaws and teeth of alligators, sharks, and barracudas were all imported from the Gulf Coast. The canine teeth of grizzly bears

were brought in from the West. Smaller items were probably used to decorate clothing or worn as personal charms, but the larger ones may have been stored as treasure and eventually buried with their owners.

Many Hopewell goods were made just for show or for use as grave offerings. The Hopewell people made fine pottery, a skill that the Adena had not mastered, and some types were used only as grave goods. Hopewell potters also made small but very realistic hu-

Cutouts of mica are found in Hopewell graves. This one, 28 centimeters (11 inches) long, represents a bird claw.

Male figurine of terra-cotta pottery found in a Hopewell burial in Hamilton County, Ohio. Hopewell men may have arranged their hair in the same topknot style as that worn by this figure.

man figurines or effigies that have told us much about Hopewell dress and hairstyles.

Hopewell carvers turned fine-grained stone into many forms, most notably the platform pipe. These pipes often have an animal figure or effigy, such as a human head, frog, toad, waterfowl, owl, hawk, raven, bear, or other animal, sitting on an arched rectangular tablet. The pipe bowl is in the head or back of the effigy.

The Hopewell created a trade network that extended to most of the continent east of the Rockies and south of the subarctic forests of Canada. The Indian communities that were the sources of the raw materials that the Hopewell demanded received and adopted the use of the finished goods in exchange, and we can trace the movement of these goods outward for as long as the trade network survived. The idea of constructing burial mounds spread even farther. Thousands of burial mounds can still be found throughout most of the Eastern Woodlands. Where Hopewell culture had particularly strong influences outside Ohio, archaeologists have often given local cultures "Hopewellian" names. There are at least 13 variants of Hopewellian culture scattered around the Eastern Woodlands, and these flourished for as long as the trade network lasted.

The Hopewell system was maintained over several centuries by the steady demand for luxury goods to be used as grave offerings. If the goods had been accumulated by the living and passed on to others when owners died, the demand would have weakened over that period of time. But even steady demand could not keep the system going indefinitely. Hopewell culture was waning by A.D. 400, and although it may have lasted until A.D. 600 in a few places, the trading network was breaking down. We still do not know why this happened. Perhaps new domesticated plants from Mexico were making possible the rise of competing cultures. Perhaps shifts in the climate weakened the ability of the Hopewell to sustain their trading system and the burial practices that depended on it.

In the upper Midwest Hopewell influences led to the cultural development now known as the Effigy Mound culture, which lasted a few centuries longer. Moundbuilders in what are now the states of Wisconsin, Minnesota, and Iowa built effigy mounds in the shapes of panthers, bears, humans, and birds. Bird effigies around Madison, Wisconsin, have huge wingspans, one of them measuring 190 meters (625 feet) from tip to tip. A human effigy near Baraboo, Wisconsin, was 65 meters (215 feet) tall before its feet were cut off by a modern road. Effigy Mound sites sometimes contain flexed primary burials, interments of individuals with their knees drawn up to their chests. The mounds often contain secondary burials, either cremations or bundles of bones gathered after the bodies had first been exposed long enough to disintegrate. Few of the Effigy Mound burials are accompanied by grave goods.

There is a 400-year gap between the disintegration of the Hopewell exchange system and the rise of the next major tradition in the Eastern Woodlands. This gap lasted from A.D. 400 to 800. People did not simply disappear for 400 years, of course. Local cultures continued to thrive, and some seem not to have noticed the decline of the Hopewell trading system. Point Peninsula culture in New York, Weeden Island culture in Florida, and Effigy Mound culture in Wisconsin all continued without interruption. In Ohio, the descendants of the Hopewell turned their building skills to the construction of true fortifications. Fort Ancient culture, as archaeologists call it, flourished in a time of increasing warfare after A.D. 800. However, the Hopewell trade network was gone and by A.D. 800 a new tradition was expanding throughout the Eastern Woodlands.

The new tradition is known as Mississippian, and it was based on the introduction of new varieties of corn from Mexico. Because the earlier varieties required long growing seasons, they could contribute only to those Indian cultures in the southernmost part of the Eastern Woodlands, in what is now the southeastern United States, where the growing season was more than 200 days long. The newer varieties included some that could do well with as few as 120 frost-free days as far north as southern Ontario. Furthermore, by around A.D. 1000 Mexican beans were added to the list of cultivated plants. Beans are high in protein and would have been an essential supplement to the protein available from wild animal sources alone, which would never have been numerous enough to meet the needs of urban centers, thus making it more possible for large populations to develop even though they had no domesticated animals. The "three sisters," maize, squash, and now beans, which complement one another in nutritive value almost perfectly, constituted the basis for North American Indian agriculture.

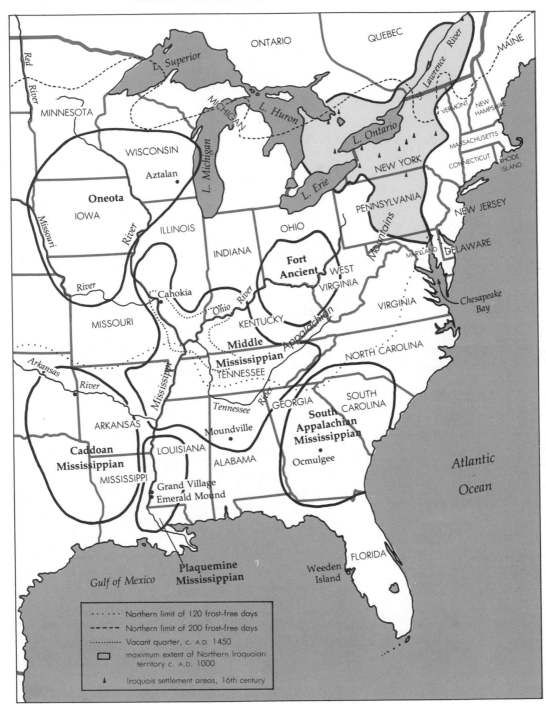

ONTARIO

QUEBEC

MAINE

L. Superior

St. Lawrence River

MINNESOTA

MICHIGAN

L. Huron

VERMONT

NEW HAMPSHIRE

WISCONSIN

L. Ontario

MASSACHUSETTS

CONNECTICUT

RHODE ISLAND

Aztalan

Oneota

L. Erie

NEW YORK

IOWA

Missouri

ILLINOIS

River

L. Michigan

OHIO

PENNSYLVANIA

NEW JERSEY

INDIANA

Fort Ancient

WEST VIRGINIA

Mountains

MARYLAND

DELAWARE

River

Cahokia

Ohio River

Chesapeake Bay

MISSOURI

KENTUCKY

VIRGINIA

Appalachian

NORTH CAROLINA

Arkansas

Middle Mississippian

TENNESSEE

River

Tennessee

River

GEORGIA

SOUTH CAROLINA

ARKANSAS

Moundville

South Appalachian Mississippian

Caddoan Mississippian

LOUISIANA

ALABAMA

Ocmulgee

Atlantic Ocean

MISSISSIPPI

Grand Village

Emerald Mound

FLORIDA

Gulf of Mexico

Plaquemine Mississippian

Weeden Island

· · · · · Northern limit of 120 frost-free days

- - - - Northern limit of 200 frost-free days

· · · · · · Vacant quarter, c. A.D. 1450

▭ maximum extent of Northern Iroquoian territory c. A.D. 1000

▲ Iroquois settlement areas, 16th century

variations in the Southeast are known as Caddoan Mississippian, Plaquemine Mississippian, and South Appalachian Mississippian. Another version, known as Oneota, developed northwest of Middle Mississippi.

Cahokia, Illinois, is the largest Middle Mississippi city known and the largest prehistoric city north of Mexico. It was founded around A.D. 600, and at its peak 600 years later it had about 10,000 inhabitants. Cahokia has more than 100 mounds, 17 of which lie within a palisaded city center. The largest is a huge structure within the palisade known as Monks Mound. Its base is an immense rectangle covering an area equivalent to 30 football fields and it stands more than 30 meters (100 feet) high. All of this was built in 14 stages by Indians carrying a basketload of earth at a time.

Moundville, Alabama, is another Middle Mississippi site. It is not as big as Cahokia, but some of the finest Mississippian art known comes from Moundville. Three ponds within the site area were apparently used to store live fish. Natural U-shaped oxbow lakes in the vicinity of Cahokia apparently served the same purpose.

Mississippian towns typically contained from 1 to 20 flat-topped temple mounds that served as platforms for ceremonial buildings or other public structures. Some of these structures were residences for the elite. The sites were often surrounded by a stockade, with residences located both inside and outside the lines of the stockade walls.

Horticulture in the surrounding fields was intensive. In some cases corn fields were planted twice in a single season; each crop was harvested while the corn was still soft and green and was eaten immediately. Other fields were planted only once a season, and the corn was allowed to ripen and dry on the stalk before being stored. Beans were planted next to the corn, their vines allowed to twine around the corn stalks for support. Squash, gourds, sunflowers, and other local domesticated plants were either planted or encouraged to grow naturally around the margins of the fields. Because deeply rooted grasses did not become established on the frequently flooded river bottomlands, digging sticks and hoes were the only tools necessary to produce large yields. In the surrounding hills, however, deeply rooted grasses kept the soil from being cultivated with simple hand tools. The ground here would remain largely uncultivated until plows and draft animals were introduced from Europe.

Mississippian farmers, unlike those in Mexico and the Southwest, did not manage water, either through irrigation or field drainage. Instead of expanding into areas where water control would have been necessary, Mississippian farmers competed for the best river bottomlands, which were periodically flooded. There is much evidence of warfare in this area. The requirements of the Mississippians for fields that were easy to cultivate led to competition for the best fields even where slightly

ARCHAEOLOGY IN IROQUOIS COUNTRY

The Southwest features prehistoric stone architecture, the Eastern Woodlands are known for their burial and temple mounds, and pit houses are found in many parts of North America. However, many prehistoric sites do not have such visible signs of human settlement. In these cases the archaeologist might be lucky to find the stains or mold left by a few long-gone upright posts in the light-colored subsoil. Archaeologists use these "post-mold" stains, along with other evidence, to determine the shape and size of houses and the living arrangements within the houses. Post-mold stains have made it possible to reconstruct larger settlement patterns in many regions, and especially in the Northeast. Here archaeologists have been able to trace the development of Iroquois communities as they increasingly depended on horticulture (for food) and became cohesive politically.

The dwellings of the late prehistoric Iroquois of the interior Northeast often left very regular and extensive house and village patterns in the earth. As a result of numerous excavations in upstate New York we know that an Iroquois longhouse at this time was typically 7 meters (23 feet) wide and as long as necessary to house the related people that lived in it. All of the women in a longhouse were members of the same clan. Every Iroquois village had from three to eight clans, but the number of houses could be as great as fifty. Each longhouse contained only one segment of one of the clans. A longhouse therefore contained related women of a particular clan, with their husbands and children. Each longhouse section was made up of two compartments that faced each other across an aisle that ran the length of

---

In North America the absence of animals suitable for domestication had caused a protein shortage, which had delayed cultural development. This major nutritional stumbling block was at last overcome by the lowly bean.

The early Mississippian period also saw the development of true hoes. The hoe, used to clear weeds and break up the soil, and a digging stick to prepare the soil for planting are all the tools needed to cultivate the three sisters. The Indians did not have draft animals; they used only simple hand-held tools to produce high yields from small numbers of seeds.

There were advances in other areas of culture too. The bow and arrow had been introduced by A.D. 1000. Their appearance might even have helped bring about the decline of the Hopewell. The spear-thrower was not completely

the longhouse. Each compartment housed an adult woman and her immediate family, typically her husband and two or three children.

Although the houses found throughout Iroquois country were built in the same way, their numbers and arrangements in villages varied according to other needs. Larger villages were surrounded by palisades, causing early Dutch and English writers to refer to them as castles. Many villages of the 16th century were located on top of steep hills for protection, the palisades often built to follow the irregular contours of the hilltop. Steep hills supplemented palisades in discouraging attackers. Later villages adopted squared palisades of a more European design, probably because straight-walled fortifications are more easily protected by gunfire from their corner bastions.

Post-mold patterns often survive even modern plowing, which usually does not go deep enough to remove the telltale stains below the topsoil. Thus even a flat field of corn can yield important information on settlements if excavated properly. The upper portions of the soil that have been disturbed by plowing must be removed carefully. In the past some archaeologists used road graders and other heavy equipment, but most modern archaeologists now direct large crews using shovels and other hand tools. Heavy equipment is destructive and village sites are rare, so hand excavation is the rule except in emergency situations when a site must be removed quickly. After the disturbed upper layer of soil is removed, the exposed undisturbed subsoil layer can be mapped. The house patterns and palisade wall of a village usually show up as rows of dark dots in the light-colored subsoil. Features such as hearths and storage pits are usually found as well. When the site map is complete, the archaeologist has a detailed picture of an Iroquois community.

abandoned at first, but it fell out of favor among hunters and warriors more interested in speed than impact, and it was forgotten by the time the first Europeans arrived.

Because of the new crops and technology, Mississippian settlements were larger and more complex than those of earlier periods. They were true towns, and sometimes even cities. Mississippian towns often had temple mounds and artifact types showing Mexican influence. This indicates that the rising Mexican civilizations were having an indirect impact on Indian cultures as far away as the Ohio Valley. The cities and towns were supported by fishing and intensive cultivation in the rich soil of the Mississippi, Ohio, Tennessee, Arkansas, and Red river valleys. The center of this development is known as Middle Mississippi culture. Regional

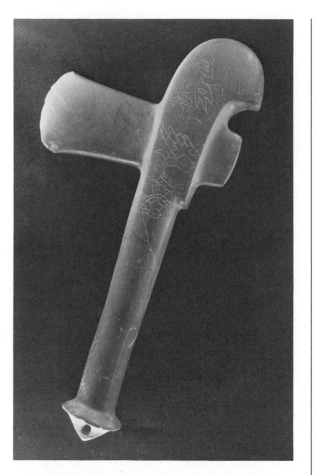

Mississippian ax carved from one piece of stone, probably used for ritual purposes, from the Etowah site in Georgia. A three-pronged forked-eye symbol appears on a human profile near the end of the haft. Etowah was a large southern Mississippian community.

less productive fields or less dependable growing seasons were available.

Mississippian societies were, apparently, ranked societies with permanent offices. Leadership in these chiefdoms was probably permanent and in some way hereditary. The large central com-munities contained a disproportionate number of elaborate public structures compared to smaller subordinate towns. The lack of such structures in the smaller towns suggests that the major centers were politically dominant over large areas. The chiefdoms at Cahokia and Moundville, two well-studied Mississippian centers, appear to have been quite complex, so much so that some scholars believe these were organized as states, with two or more levels of political offices. State organization would involve standing armies and bureaucratic institutions, both of which are difficult to detect by archaeological means. Future research may solve the question of state organization.

Mississippian artifacts include polished stone axes, bowls, and pipes. Both the handle and bit of the axes are often carved from a single piece of dense stone. The pottery shows that shaping, stamping, and incising of the wet clay continued to be the principal techniques for decorating, as in earlier periods, but new ideas appeared in the form of pots shaped like human heads (probably representing war trophies), long-necked water jugs, round-bottomed pots, and other forms suggesting Mexican influences. Later Mississippian sites sometimes contain painted vessels, rare in the Eastern Woodlands. Many of these are painted in two colors; some are decorated with negative painting. This technique involves coating the pot with a base color and then painting on a wax coating in the desired design. The vessel is then coated with a second color. When the pot is baked to harden the clay, the wax melts and carries away with it all of the second color applied over it, thus the first color shows through where the wax design was applied.

Shell carving was also important to the Mississippians. Whole conches or shell disks were incised with characteristic designs. A series of very specific motifs are found engraved on shells in sites across the southern Mississippian region. This complex of motifs, rare in Middle Mississippian sites, has come to be known as the Southern Cult and is considered a variant of the Mississippian culture. Common motifs are a sunburst, an elaborate cross, a human eye in the palm of an open hand, arrows with lobes attached on both sides, a forked eye (angular designs next to the eye), a weeping eye, and several abstract designs. Although these motifs are most commonly seen on engraved shells, they also occur on wood, carved stone, chipped stone, painted textiles, and embossed native copper sheets. The Southern Cult shows some Mexican influence but also elements of Hopewell and other Eastern Woodlands cultures. Objects bearing the motifs of the Southern Cult appear most frequently at large sites and are clearly related to ceremonies conducted on and around the large earthen temple mounds. The cult did not become fully elaborated until after A.D. 1000 and was still flourishing when Spanish explorer Hernando de Soto arrived in 1541.

The southeastern Mississippians were among the first North Americans to be devastated by epidemics of dis-

eases brought to the continent by Europeans. As a consequence, much of what we might otherwise know about the Southern Cult died out with its practitioners before it could be recorded. A notable exception to this is Natchez, a center of the Plaquemine Mississippian. French explorers visited Grand Village and Emerald Mound while the Plaquemine Mississippian was still functioning, and the descrip-

Unique designs engraved on shell marked the southern variant of Mississippian culture. This male figure decorates the cuplike end of a shell. It is from a burial mound at the Spiro site in Oklahoma, where stone, copper, and pottery artifacts have also been found.

A stone disk carved with an eye in the center of an open human hand, surrounded by two intertwined rattlesnakes. These designs are typical of the Southern Cult.

tions they provided (1718–34) have often been used by archaeologists to describe the activities that probably went on at Mississippian sites.

Middle Mississippi and Oneota sites were apparently constructed by the ancestors of Siouan-speaking Indians, some of whom still live in the region. Curiously, there may have been an ex-

panding depopulated "vacant quarter," an area that had become uninhabited, in the heartland of Middle Mississippi by A.D. 1450. This is much too early for the population to have disappeared as a consequence of European diseases. Instead, a population collapse or at least serious decline seems to have been caused by indigenous factors.

New evidence comes from research by physical anthropologists who specialize in the study of human bone remains. In bones from sites in this region, they have found evidence of tuberculosis and other diseases related to early urban crowding and the absence of efficient waste disposal systems. Their work suggests that most preindustrial cities in the New World were large and socially attractive urban centers but fundamentally unhealthy. Tuberculosis, a native ailment, spread rapidly where human living conditions were crowded and relatively permanent. The disease was only one of several ailments—many of which involved endemic intestinal parasites—that flourish under such conditions. Because of the high rates of illness and mortality, it is likely that preindustrial cities depended upon a steady flow of immigrants to replenish their continually ravaged populations. Without new, healthy arrivals, the cities would experience population deficits. That is apparently what happened to the Middle Mississippi cities at the core of the region. Their collapse can be seen as the natural result of the depletion of the pool of potential immigrants in the hinterlands.

To the northeast, Fort Ancient culture and various Iroquoian and Algonquian cultures went their own way. Middle Mississippi culture was militarily and politically expansive, however, and colonies from the heartland have been found in other areas. Aztalan, Wisconsin, is a Middle Mississippi town in the territory of Oneota culture. Ocmulgee, Georgia, is a Middle Mississippi site in South Appalachian Mississippian territory. It seems likely that Mississippian cultures outside the heartland were stimulated to develop at least partly by these intrusive colonies, sent out from and managed by the major centers. Over some time, the culture probably spread among smaller unrelated groups in the colonized areas. By 1450 the political and economic systems in the core area of Middle Mississippi were in trouble, and after that date many of the major centers were abandoned. Ironically, many of the subsidiary centers that were stimulated to develop in outlying areas throughout the region continued to thrive until the arrival of European explorers. De Soto, for example, visited several such Mississippian centers in his journey through the Southeast. ▲

Excavation of Wilson Butte rock shelter in Idaho, one of the oldest Paleo-Indian sites in North America.

THE
PREHISTORY
OF THE
WEST

The American West is made up of many different environments. Some of them provide abundant natural food for people, while others seem to offer only harsh living conditions. The West is defined here as including the Great Plains. The Far West comprises the huge area that lies west of the Great Plains, the Southwest, and the interior forests of Canada. The Far West is bounded by mountain ranges to the east and ocean shores to the west.

The Rocky Mountain chain sets off the Far West from the Great Plains to the east. A second chain of western mountain ranges consists of the Sierra Nevada in eastern California and the Cascade Range of Oregon, Washington, and British Columbia. Between these two great chains of mountains lies a region called the Desert West. This in turn is made up of three subregions: the Southwest, the Great Basin, and the Plateau. (Because of its special importance to archaeology, the Southwest is discussed in a separate chapter.)

The Great Basin lies just north of the Southwest subregion, primarily in the modern states of Nevada and Utah. The rivers of the Great Basin flow inward, down from the mountain ranges that surround the region. Some of the water soaks into the dry landscape, some evaporates, and some ends up in shallow salty lakes. The largest of these is the Great Salt Lake of Utah. Nowhere do the rivers of the Great Basin break through the mountains to run westward to the sea. What little rain falls in the Great Basin and reaches the shallow lakes accumulates there until it evaporates. Before modern transportation and irrigation systems were introduced, the scarcity of water in the Great Basin allowed for the growth of only enough food to support a thin population of hunters and gatherers.

The most notable attempt by prehistoric Indians to bring farming and settled life to the Great Basin was the expansion of Fremont culture into Utah sometime after A.D. 400. Fremont was basically a Southwest culture. Archaeologists are still uncertain whether it was adopted by local hunters and gatherers or carried in by migrants from the Southwest. In the Great Basin, the Fremont people's fields dried up and their villages were abandoned around A.D. 1300. We do not know who their modern descendants might be, if any survived at all.

The hunters and gatherers responsible for most of the prehistory of the Great Basin have been studied through the excavation of many dry cave sites. Danger Cave and Hogup Cave in northwestern Utah illustrate the long prehistoric sequences archaeologists have found at such sites. These caves contain durable remains such as projectile points, grinding stones, and bone tools. But they have also preserved fragments of nets, coiled and twined basketry, and other fiber artifacts. Archaeologists have been able to reconstruct prehistoric diets from preserved bones, seeds, and even the contents of human waste. Remains of bison, antelope, sheep, and deer are sometimes found, but those of small rodents, hares, and rabbits are more common. Waterfowl and shore birds are found in cave deposits that date to the periods just following the demise of Paleo-Indians around 8000 B.C., but they were not common after 1200 B.C. This indicates that marshlands were drying up and that an environment that was already harsh became increasingly difficult for human communities over a long period of time.

Historical documents show that into the 19th century people living in the Great Basin often moved seasonally from stream-bank camps on the valley floors to pinyon groves on the mountain slopes. Pinyon nuts were gathered in the fall, stored, and eaten through the winter. Archaeology has shown that this practice dates back to at least 2500 B.C.

After Fremont culture disappeared, the Great Basin was taken over by the Shoshone, Ute, Paiute, and related peoples. They expanded northeastward out of a core area in the desert of what are now southeastern California and southern Nevada. After Spaniards introduced horses in the colonial Southwest in the late 16th century, these cultures became nomads on horseback, and eventually introduced the practice of mounted nomadism to the Great Plains. The use of horses spread rapidly beginning in the 17th century. Although their use spread mainly from the Southwest and in the Great Basin, they had their greatest impact on the cultures of the Great Plains. Indian cultures were profoundly transformed wherever the horse was taken up as a new mode of transportation, soon becoming as indispensable as the automobile is today. On the Great Plains and elsewhere, the horse almost immediately became the most important form of property a person could own, giving bands of nomads greater freedom and mobility than they had ever enjoyed previously.

The Plateau is the third subregion of the Desert West. It lies north of the Great Basin, mainly in the interior of what are now the states of Oregon and Washington and the province of British Columbia. More rain falls here than farther south, and the streams of the Plateau collect into two major rivers that flow through the Cascade Mountain range west to the Pacific Ocean. These major rivers, the Columbia and the Fraser, provide spawning streams for Pacific salmon and other fish. Consequently, the prehistoric people of the Plateau had important food resources in their rivers that the people of the Great Basin lacked. By the first few centuries A.D., many of the people of the Plateau had settled in villages, where they lived in earth lodges for at least

part of the year. Such villages indicate that the cultures of the Plateau were able to collect and store enough food each year to maintain fairly large and almost permanent communities.

The Far West, in contrast to the dry interior Desert West, is a long strip of coast that is dry in the south but becomes wetter as one moves northward. The long, dry Mexican peninsula of Baja California is isolated from the rest of North America by the Gulf of California. California is the middle portion of the Far West. Although not vast, it contains an extraordinary amount of environmental diversity. Some of this is the result of variation between the hot south and the cooler conditions that prevail 1100 kilometers (680 miles) to the north. Some environmental diver-

An earth lodge of the Hidatsa tribe, photographed in the early 20th century. Earth-lodge villages were semipermanent communities of the people who lived on the Plateau and Great Plains regions after A.D. 1000.

sity results from variations in elevation from sea level to 4400 meters (14,400 feet). Some of it results from the mountains, which cause heavy rains to fall on their western slopes while shielding interior dry valleys from moisture. Consequently, in California there are thick redwood forests, open oak parklands, deserts, vast tracts of scrub, and other equally distinctive environments. These conditions discouraged prehistoric Californians from adopting even the simple cultivation of the Southwest, and they promoted the tendency for communities to live within small territories. The plants available for cultivation would have had to be adapted to each local environment and in most cases would not have been obviously superior to the wild food resources that were already locally available. The agricultural potential of California would not be realized until the 19th century, when new cultivation techniques and transportation allowed farmers to make use of this environmental diversity.

Bedrock mortars (grinding pits) for preparation of acorn meal. In much of California, acorns were an important dietary staple from about 2000 B.C. to recent times. Acorns must be carefully prepared to remove a poisonous substance; then the acorns must be ground into a meal before they can be cooked.

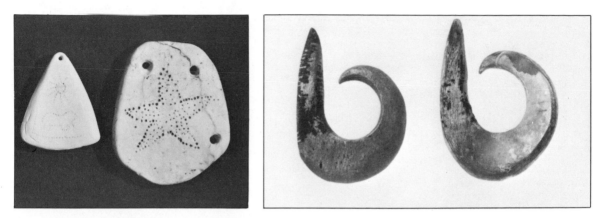

Among the luxury goods produced by the prehistoric Indians living along the Pacific Coast in California were (right) carved abalone-shell fishhooks, and (left) drilled-shell pendants. These, made by the Chumash, were traded to people living inland for objects made of stone.

Prehistoric California attracted and accommodated immigrants of many backgrounds. Small bands drifted in at various times from nearly every direction but west (the Pacific Ocean). There were an unusual number of separate language families. Indians from many backgrounds adapted in small groups to many different California environments, forming a complex mosaic of languages and cultures.

Even though all California cultures maintained a hunting and foraging way of life and did not practice horticulture, the region had a relatively dense population when the first Europeans arrived. How this unusual situation of dense population and rich cultural variation developed without agriculture or complicated political systems is still being investigated by archaeologists. By 2000 B.C., California Indians were beginning to make effective use of the re-

sources found in abundance in each specific environment. In one locale the primary resource might be acorns, in another sea mammals, in still another fish. By A.D. 500 this process had produced about 500 specialized small tribes, each of which had adapted to exploit the specific resources of its unique local habitat. The production of food surpluses and storage, trade, and redistribution of those surpluses were all well developed. This allowed the Indians to deal with both predictable seasonal food shortages as well as unexpected shortages resulting from drought, fire, infestations, or other natural causes. The people probably organized food production teams to harvest acorns, catch fish, trap rabbits, or take advantage of some other local resource. They could store surplus food either for the community's own use or for trade with another community fac-

ing a temporary shortage. Shell money was used as a means to make the system work more efficiently. Like modern money, it held value with which food or other items could be purchased at a later date. The complexity of the environment made it possible to trade surplus food with neighboring groups even though the only means of transporting goods were in canoes and with backpacks. Such trading systems are not possible in regions where there are long distances and little environmental diversity.

In other parts of the world where extreme environmental diversity made possible similar patterns of surplus food production and redistribution, regional political systems such as chiefdoms, nation-states, and even empires often developed. It may be unusual that these types of political organization did not develop in California. Or it may be that archaeologists simply do not yet understand cultural systems well enough to make sense of prehistoric California.

The 500 cultures that made up California by the end of the prehistoric period differed from each other in many ways, but they shared some similarities as well. Each community was usually led by a local male leader. Kinship was an important means of organization, and gifts were given to reinforce relationships. There was an active network for trading foods from an area of abundance to another where it was in short supply. Another type of food or special luxury items might have been received in exchange. The complexity of California environments produced a wide variety of luxury goods. These provide a very large and confusing series of specific artifact types for the archaeologist to analyze. Beads, pendants, fishhooks, and other items made of shell moved inland from coastal cultures. Interior cultures produced stone objects such as mortars, milling stones, and projectile points. Cultures throughout the region produced their own distinctive forms of basketry, made from local plant fibers. The people of California never acquired pottery-making skills from the cultures of the Southwest. Strange objects known to archaeologists as charm stones come in many forms, adding to the confusion. These stones often have abstract geometric shapes but no known practical use; to say that they may have had ceremonial functions brings us no closer to understanding their uses. There is still much left to understand about California prehistory.

The Northwest Coast extends from northern California along the coasts of Oregon, Washington, and British Co-

A Haida village, Queen Charlotte Island, British Columbia, late 19th century. The people of the Northwest Coast built homes, canoes, and the memorial statues known as totem poles from planks and trunks of cedar, which were abundant in forests near their villages.

Along the Northwest Coast of North America, from northern California to the Alaskan pan-
handle, people from prehistoric to recent times could depend on a variety of foods from the sea.
They often carved steatite (soapstone) representations of whales and other creatures. They had
only stone tools until, in late prehistoric times, they found iron washed ashore from shipwrecks
and used it to make sharper tools.

lumbia to the long panhandle of Alaska. There is much less environmental diversity there than in California. Mountains near the coast concentrate the rains there and produce a cool rain forest along the entire strip from Alaska to the northern border of California. Warm ocean currents and foggy air drench the coast in misty rainfall from fall until spring. The rivers fill with salmon and other migrating fish during spring and summer. In prehistoric times the thick forests provided game and wood, while the sea offered seals, whales, and other sources of food. Although the Northwest Coast environments were not as diverse as those of California, the region was nearly as rich in usable resources. Consequently, there were settled communities here by

the end of prehistory, even though agriculture was unknown.

Early Indian cultures had moved into the Northwest Coast from the interior by at least 7700 B.C. Earlier sites may have been lost to archaeologists because they were covered by rising sea levels. Over the centuries the use of shellfish led to the gradual accumulation of large shell middens. These are refuse heaps of discarded shell, a material that is well preserved even in wet environments. The shell, in turn, often preserves other discarded objects such as bone and wood that might otherwise have disappeared. Bone and ground slate implements begin to appear by 3500 B.C. Stone labrets (lip plugs), stone clubs, and spear points made of slate with edges sharpened by grinding were common by around 2000 years ago. Since then, Northwest Coast cultures have subsisted by harvesting fish runs, hunting sea mammals, and collecting shellfish, in addition to their practice of the same types of fishing and hunting activities as the neighboring cultures on the Plateau. With so many food resources, the people of the Northwest Coast were able to live in nearly permanent settlements. The giant cedar trees of the region provided straight trunks that Indians learned to split into planks using only antler wedges and heavy stone hammers. The trees were felled with stone axes and controlled burning. No prehistoric Indian craftsmen had steel saws: They used only stone and bone tools on the cedar planks that were the principal building materials for Northwest Coast houses. Dugout canoes were also built in larger and larger sizes, burned out with controlled fires and further hollowed with stone adzes. By the end of prehistory, Northwest Coast war parties were raiding neighboring coastal villages in fleets of war canoes and harpooning whales on the open sea.

With so much natural wealth along the Northwest Coast, it should not be surprising that prehistoric societies there came to focus on the accumulation of goods. This emphasis on wealth was established by A.D. 500. The natural wealth of the environment produced huge food surpluses, but the environment was so uniform and the range of foods so great that trade in basic necessities never developed in the region.

There was a tendency for upstream and downstream kin living on individual river systems to exchange goods, but beyond that kind of trade, most local cultures remained independent of one another.

In such a rich environment, everyone could accumulate large amounts of surplus food. That in turn promoted the accumulation of luxury goods. Skilled men and women turned out luxury goods to enrich their clans and promote themselves among the competitive societies of the region. Beautiful Chilkat blankets were made from mountain sheep wool and cedar bark fiber. Pipes, spoons, and other portable artifacts were made from combinations of horn, shell, copper, wood, and bone. In late prehistoric times, the people living along the Northwest Coast began to find iron in wreckage that occasionally floated to their shores from across the Pacific. Local craftsmen quickly learned to turn the iron into woodworking tools. These in turn made possible intricate carving, resulting in the development of the totem poles and other carved wooden monuments for which the peoples of the Northwest Coast cultures are still renowned. The totem poles, carved boxes, house poles, boats, and masks of this region were therefore a late development. Woodcarving replaced much of the earlier stone carving, and carved wooden objects joined other goods as indicators of wealth and rank.

Eventually the accumulation of property and its use to denote rank led to the development of the gift-giving feast known as the potlatch, described by numerous visitors to the area in historic times. This ceremony had several forms, but a common theme was the extravagant giving of valuable gifts to guests in a demonstration of the wealth and high rank of the host family. Sometimes goods were deliberately burned or broken to make this point. Piles of blankets, boxes of oil, copper plaques, and even human slaves were sometimes ritually destroyed to prove that a family had "money to burn."

East of the Rocky Mountains and stretching to the valley of the Mississippi River across the center of the North American continent is the broad grassland we know as the Great Plains.

This was the home of the bison, pronghorn antelope, mule deer, white-tailed deer, elk, black bear, and grizzly bear. All of these species are still present, but they live in small refuges, much like those descendants of the Indians who once hunted them who live on reservations.

Within this vast grassy range there are differing environments. The western plains have higher altitudes and shorter grasses. The northern and southern parts of the short-grass plains differ because of the harsher winters in the north. The lower and wetter eastern plains are dominated by taller grasses. Many refer to this region as prairie to distinguish it from the drier western plains.

A bowl of cedarwood decorated with inlaid pieces of shell for use at a potlatch. It was made by Kwakiutl people of Vancouver Island late in the 19th century.

RIVER BASIN SURVEYS

In the years following World War II, the federal government constructed a series of large dams across the Missouri River. From the time these dams were in the planning stages, it was clear that the reservoirs that would fill up behind them would cover and destroy hundreds of important archaeological sites, some of them very large villages. In 1945, the National Park Service, the Smithsonian Institution, the Army Corps of Engineers, and the Bureau of Reclamation agreed to salvage as much as possible of these archaeological remains. This large and complex interagency salvage program came to be known as the River Basin Surveys.

Sites threatened by dam construction were located, mapped, photographed, and often partly excavated. By 1969, major excavations had been carried out at 96 sites in the Missouri River valley of North and South Dakota alone.

The River Basin Surveys program marked a new beginning for large-scale public archaeology in the United States. There had been earlier large-scale archaeological efforts by Works Progress Administration (WPA) crews of the Great Depression era, but these had often involved untrained crews and lacked professional supervision. By 1970, the River Basin Surveys program was being phased out, but there was a growing awareness of the need for an even larger effort in public archaeology. The construction of interstate highways was destroying uncounted numbers of archaeological sites, and other kinds of construction were destroying irreplaceable archaeological remains in the name of progress. The concerns of professional and amateur archaeologists were heard in Washington, and laws passed in the middle of the 1970s expanded public archaeology once again.

Now any project supported by federal money must carry out an archaeological survey in advance. If significant remains are found, additional work must be carried out to avoid them, or to salvage them if they cannot be avoided. Many states and local governments have adopted similar regulations. As a result there are now many public archaeology projects, and consequently many opportunities for archaeologists. At the same time, the archaeological evidence of the earliest Americans is no longer written off as an expendable cost of progress. What remains to us now is all that we will ever have, and modern public archaeology ensures that we use it carefully.

The next step will be to involve the public more in sharing both the workload and the benefits of public archaeology. Volunteer participation in projects could be much greater than it now is, and so could the resulting benefits of museum display and publication. Schools, colleges, museums, and local governments would all profit from following the example of interagency cooperation first seen in the River Basin Surveys program.

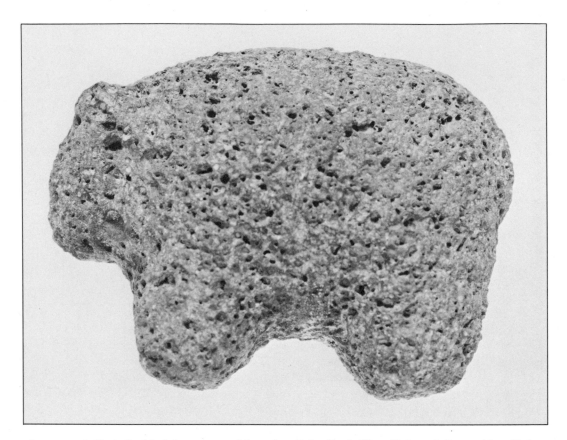

A representation of a black bear, carved from basalt by the Indians living at the rapids called the Dalles on the Columbia River in Oregon.

There were many food resources for early hunters and gatherers on the Great Plains. Unlike the abundance in California and the Northwest Coast, the food sources on the Plains were not concentrated within limited geographic areas. People living on the Plains had to follow herds of game animals and gather widely scattered plant foods in the right seasons wherever they occurred. Such conditions guaranteed that early Indian cultures on the Plains would be nomadic.

Farming was possible on the Great Plains, especially along the streams that flow eastward from the Rockies to join the Mississippi River. But because of periodic drought and deeply rooted grasses, farming was so difficult that the Archaic cultures on the Plains did not adopt and develop it. Instead, the practice of agriculture, which was developed first in the Eastern Woodlands, was then brought to the Plains by farmers from the East who were already skilled in planting and tending crops.

In a few cases, people from the Southwest also drifted onto the Plains, bringing farming skills with them. But most of the later cultural developments on the Great Plains came from the East.

The popular image of a Plains Indian is the warrior in feathered headdress and on horseback. But this version of Plains Indian culture was only the last brief chapter in a long development. The horse species native to the Americas died out with other large game animals at the end of the Ice Age 10,000 years ago. The mustangs and Indian ponies of the historic Great Plains were introduced by Spanish colonists in the Southwest. Indians on the Plains did not use horses for transportation before the 1600s. But in the century following the reintroduction of the horse, one Indian nation after another discovered the advantages offered by this new means of transportation. They could now hunt the huge bison herds more efficiently. They could travel the long distances between patches of natural plant foods in less time than before, when they had to go on foot. This meant that the Plains people could put aside the risky business of farming for the more exciting and productive life of hunting and herding. In only a few decades, many permanent villages in the prairie valleys were abandoned, and nomadic tipi villages became the most common kind of settlement on the Great Plains. The tipi was a portable home made of animal hide. It could be dismantled, neatly packed for travel, and erected again in a new village in a short time.

Pastoralism—keeping herds of livestock—had become possible in Asia only after farmers there had domesticated horses, cattle, and the grains to feed them. Similarly, in North America, pastoralism was a spinoff of animal domestication and earlier farming. In North America the key animal, the horse, was imported, because there was no equivalent on the continent. The key meat-producing animal was the bison (or buffalo) rather than the cattle or yak of Europe and Asia. Bison resist domestication, so Indian hunters could not become true herders. Yet in the Southwest sheep were adopted quickly by the Navajo after being introduced by the Spaniards, and cattle might eventually have been adopted on the Plains in the same way. Had it not been for the epidemics that depopulated these and other Indian nations, it is also likely that the Plains Indians would have eventually duplicated the nomadic conquests seen earlier in Asia. Just as the Mongols and others swept westward from the grasslands of central Asia and across the farmlands of western Asia and Eastern Europe, the Plains Indians might have swept eastward across the native farmlands of the Eastern Woodlands. But disease and warfare prevented such a conquest from taking place.

Early hunter-gatherers on the Great Plains were not numerous. Eastern Woodlands people moving westward up the river valleys probably met with very little resistance. The first farmers from the East came into the prairie river valleys between 250 B.C. and A.D. 950. This is called the Plains Woodland period. These settlers were influenced by Hopewell cultures. The Kansas City Hopewellian was established near the modern city. It appears that maize was one of the crops grown by these prairie Hopewellian people, even though it had not yet become important in the Eastern Woodlands. Hopewell pottery and artifacts of native copper, obsidian, and stone indicate that the people in this area were participating in Hopewell trade. However, it is still not certain what these communities were trading in exchange. It may be that the route for the Yellowstone obsidian and North Dakota chalcedony, which were imported by Ohio Hopewell artisans, was down the Missouri River, and that the trade was controlled by the Kansas City Hopewellians. Rather than producing something, perhaps they were just middlemen in the trading network.

Woodland-type burial mounds extend west from the Eastern Woodlands to the eastern Dakotas and southern Manitoba, Canada. A Plains flavor was

Excavating a Kansas City Hopewell site.

added to this eastern tradition by the burial of bison skeletons or skulls in many mounds. The idea of constructing burial mounds spread into the northern Plains through Minnesota. In this area there occurred a spinoff of Hopewell similar to the Effigy Mound tradition of Wisconsin. The people responsible were probably the ancestors of the historic Dakota (Sioux), Assiniboin, and Cheyenne Indians.

Although evidence of Woodland farming communities is sometimes found farther west on the Plains, the general picture is one of a continuing Archaic way of life over most of the region. Archaic hunting and gathering, and particularly the practice of communal bison hunting, continued through and after the 1100-year-long Plains Woodland period on much of the Plains.

The bow and arrow were introduced as new hunting weapons late in the Plains Woodland period, which ended around A.D. 950. The source was probably the Athapascan hunters of western Canada, who had in turn received the new weapons from the Eskimos. The bow and arrow might even have contributed to the ability of Northern Athapascans to expand southward through the western Plains. The descendants of those who eventually reached the Southwest became the modern Navajo and Apache.

The Plains Woodland period was followed by the Plains Village period, which lasted in some places until 1850, well into historic times. This new wave

Squash was sliced and dried in the sun by the Hidatsa and other Plains Indians and strung on cord for storage, to be used during the winter. About 1,000 years ago, horticulture began to supplement food derived from hunting and gathering on the Plains. Plains Village cultures planted corn, beans, and squash.

of colonization consisted of people spreading westward from large Mississippian centers in the Eastern Woodlands. They built new Plains Village towns that were larger and more permanent than the Plains Woodland communities had been. Some were even fortified by dry moats and stockades. The houses were permanent lodges, large enough to hold several related families.

The farming system of the Plains Village people involved strains of maize and beans that matured more rapidly than previous varieties, as well as other plants. These advanced crops were basically the same as those that fueled the rise of Mississippian cultures in the Eastern Woodlands. The Mississippian centers of the East were large chiefdoms, sometimes even states. But the river-bottom farming of the Plains Villagers could not support such advanced political systems. The small Plains Village colonies may well have been as independent as the pioneer towns of non-Indian settlers that sprang up in the same places after 1800.

Many of the best known Plains Village sites lie in the valley of the Missouri River. Sites of the Middle Missouri tradition are found mostly along the Missouri River in what are now the states of North and South Dakota. A severe drought near the end of the period forced the surviving Middle Missouri villagers to gather along a smaller stretch of the Missouri River valley, where they would eventually become the historic Hidatsa and Mandan.

Plains Village sites dating to A.D. 1000–1400 constitute the Central Plains tradition. People's houses were scattered in small unfortified clusters along river bluffs. The drought appears to have forced them to abandon many villages during the 13th century, particularly those that were situated farther west on the drier High Plains. The Central Plains villagers moved back downstream and came together to form what archaeologists call the Coalescent (coming-together) tradition. Some of them spread up the Missouri between 1450 and 1680. These people, now known as the Arikara, joined the Mandan and Hidatsa in the Middle Missouri area. Their close relatives, the Pawnee, remained behind.

As the prehistoric period came to an end, many of the farming Plains people acquired horses. They abandoned their settled way of life to become mounted nomads like the earlier Plains hunters. The cultures of the Great Plains changed quickly with the arrival of the horse. Oneota villagers became the Siouan-speaking tribes known historically as the Oto, Missouri, and Iowa. Similarly, the Wichita split off from the Caddoan Mississippian in the Southeast, and the Crow split off from the Hidatsa. Many other communities left the river valleys to hunt bison on horseback at least part-time. In the North, various Dakota, Assiniboin, and Cheyenne peoples moved out of settled villages and into nomadic tipi villages on the Plains. The ancestors of the Arapaho, Blackfeet, Nez Perce, Comanche, Kiowa, and some Shoshone and Apache abandoned hunting and gathering on foot to become mounted nomads. In the end, the people of the Mandan, Hidatsa, and Arikara were the exception among Plains cultures; they remained in their villages and traded the corn they raised for bison meat brought in by nomads.

Medicine wheel of boulders in the Bighorn Mountains, Wyoming.

But the nomadic horseback-riding hunters of the Plains did not survive very long as independent cultures. They were almost immediately in competition with European cultures moving westward from the East. The nomads left few outstanding sites behind. The exceptions are the large and impressive spoked circles of boulders known as medicine wheels that are scattered from Wyoming to Alberta, Canada. The largest of these is a 28-spoked circle in the Bighorn Mountains of Wyoming. These monuments often appear to be oriented toward the rising point of the sun on the longest day of the year, the summer solstice. The sig-nificance of these structures was probably primarily ceremonial, along with the political and social significance that usually accompanies ceremony in human society. It is tempting to point to the similarities between the medicine wheels of prehistoric times and the temporary structures erected by Plains Indians in the 19th century for their Sun Dance ceremonies. But the Sun Dance was a ceremony unique to its period, in part an expression of masculine ideals of the mounted nomadic way of life that was no more. The historic Sun Dance might be related to the prehistoric medicine wheels in only the most general way. ▲

Excavation of a house at an Eskimo site in the Katmai National Park and Preserve, Alaska.

THE
ESKIMOS
AND THEIR
ANCESTORS

The Arctic is a severe environment for all living things. Bands of human hunters penetrated its northernmost limits only near the end of prehistory, and their numbers never grew very large. The region does not simply consist of those parts of North America north of the Arctic Circle. An accurate definition is more complicated than that, and must involve environment as well as geography. True, much of North America's Arctic land does lie north of the Arctic Circle, and as a consquence there are nights without darkness in the summer and days without light in the winter. But much of the American Arctic also lies south of the Arctic Circle.

Like the tip of Siberia facing it across the Bering Strait, the west coast of Alaska is mostly treeless tundra. Tundra also stretches across northern Alaska and Canada, including the Arctic islands of Canada. However, the coastal band of tundra also dips southward below the Arctic Circle to fringe Hudson Bay and the coast of northern Quebec and Labrador. All of Greenland is ringed by tundra, even the part south of the Arctic Circle. On land, the Arctic was once the private domain of the polar bear.

The Arctic is also a seascape. The bays and inlets of the Arctic Ocean give the tundra a ragged icy border and provide an environment for the sea mammals of the region. Beluga whales and other whale species are found throughout much of the Arctic Ocean. Bearded and ringed seals are even more widely distributed. Walrus, less widespread, are often found off the shores prowled by the polar bear. For much of the year the Arctic Ocean is clogged with pack ice, making it difficult to distinguish the snow-covered land from the sea. In some periods of prehistory the pack ice retreated for decades at a time, allowing the whales to spread and increase in numbers, and tempting human communities to spread northward as well. In other periods the pack ice closed off vast areas to both game and humans, sometimes putting a tragic end to human bands that ventured too far.

This, then, is the environment that remained vacant of human bands for thousands of years but was eventually conquered by the ancestors of the Eskimos. We know that early hunters came from Asia to the Americas through what is now Alaska. Groups of later migrants occasionally used the same route. Many of the earliest migrants probably lived on the broad areas of the continental shelf that are now submerged but were exposed when sea levels were lowered during the Ice Age. These areas are now out of reach for archaeologists. The early populations must have been small and scattered, and if their way of life kept them close to the coast, now covered by the Pacific Ocean, the meager evidence they left behind may never be found.

Archaeologists generally agree that the Eskimos and the Aleuts, who speak closely related languages, are comparative newcomers to the Americas. They arrived thousands of years after the waves of earlier ancestors of American Indians, but still long before Europeans began sending ships across the Atlantic Ocean. Early ancestors of the Eskimos were probably living in what is now Alaska by around 1000 B.C., and their Aleut relatives were probably living in what are now the Aleutian Islands off the southern coast of Alaska by this time as well.

It is possible that Eskimos were living in North America prior to this time, but it is not certain. There is, then, at least 10,000 years of Arctic prehistory, from the earliest migration perhaps 12,000 or more years ago until the arrival of Aleuts and Eskimos that does not necessarily involve the Eskimos or their direct ancestors. For most of this time their ancestors were probably living somewhere in northeastern Siberia.

For a while, finds at the Old Crow site in Yukon Territory, were thought to be more than 12,000 years old (see Chapter 2). But now that this evidence has been put in doubt, the oldest certain evidence of human habitation in the Arctic comes from several finds of stone-tool assemblages dated between 9000–6000 B.C. An assemblage is a collection of artifacts excavated from a specific site, in this case sites such as the Gallagher Flint Station in northern Alaska. Assemblages of this period are generally referred to as the American Paleo-Arctic tradition. The assemblages contain stone cores, blades (slivers of stone struck from the cores), and microblades (small sharp blades). These are found with the bones of animal species that are still in the area today as well as with some examples of horse, bison, and elk that no longer live in this region. Curiously, these are the earliest sites known in Alaska. Archaeologists have still not found the remains of Paleo-Indians or their ancestors there but strongly suspect that they must have passed through the region on their way to the more hospitable environments farther south.

A tradition that is related to the American Paleo-Arctic but different in distinctive ways has been identified on the Aleutian island of Anangula. Due

Pack ice covers the Arctic Ocean and other far northern waterways for much of the year, breaking up only in the summer.

to its location, the Anangula tradition may already have been making greater use of coastal resources than the contemporaneous American Paleo-Arctic tradition. The stone tools found at all sites from both of these traditions are similar in style to those found at sites in the interior of Siberia. As a result of the similarities, some archaeologists refer to all early materials from both sides of the Bering Strait as belonging to a single Beringian tradition.

By 4000 B.C. hunters along the Alaskan coast were certainly making use of marine resources that were not available to hunters in the interior. The people living inland had made a whole series of distinct adaptations to the resources of the region. Stone tools in-

dicating these adaptations have been found at the Onion Portage site in what is now central Alaska and at other locations both on the tundra and in forests. Despite the variations in specific stone tool styles, there is enough consistency over the whole region to allow us to consider the whole interior development as a Northern Archaic tradition. Some archaeologists think that this tradition derived from earlier Paleo-Indian developments that spread back northward into Alaska from known sites in central North America. Others believe that it developed in place out of the previous American Paleo-Arctic tradition. It may be that the people responsible for the Northern Archaic tradition were ancestors of speakers of

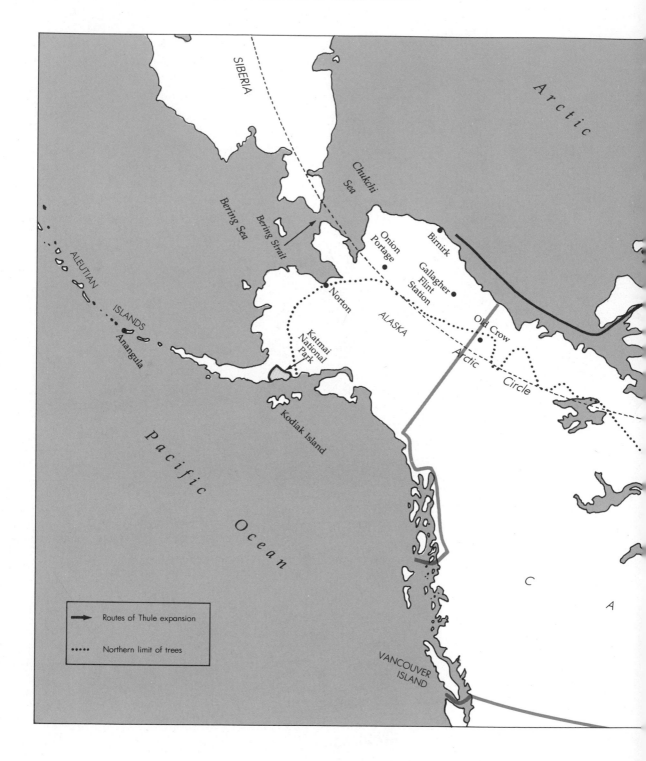

SIBERIA

Arctic

Chukchi
Sea

Bering
Sea

Bering Strait

ALEUTIAN
ISLANDS

Anangula

Birnirk

Onion
Portage

Gallagher
Flint
Station

Old Crow

Norton

ALASKA

Arctic

Circle

Katmai
National
Park

Kodiak Island

Pacific

Ocean

C

A

VANCOUVER
ISLAND

→   Routes of Thule expansion

·····   Northern limit of trees

Pit house similar to those built by the Eskimos of the Arctic Small Tool tradition reconstructed at Katmai National Park and Preserve. About 5 meters (15 feet) in diameter, the round house had a covered entry about 2 meters (6 feet) long. There was a smoke hole in the center of the low timbered roof and a hearth on the floor below it.

the historic Na-dene languages of western North America. Historically, these peoples are known by names such as Chipewyan, Kutchin, and Sarsee. However, there are other possibilities as well, and there is as yet little agreement among archaeologists.

New traditions arrived in the western Arctic between 2500 and 1900 B.C., appearing first in northern Alaska and in the Aleutian Islands. Some of the new people moved westward into the Aleutians from the Alaska Peninsula. They most likely came from Siberia and probably spoke a language that was ancestral to today's Eskimo-Aleut family of languages. Modern Eskimo languages are distantly but clearly related to Aleut, and their separation from each other appears to date to this period. The early division tells us that the Aleuts were already exclusively island people whereas the Eskimos were adapted to the mainland coast and the interior.

In this period, some people took up the manufacture of distinctive polished slate tools along the coast. The early use of this specialized technology extended from Kodiak Island eastward and southward along the Northwest Coast as far as Vancouver Island. Just how these people might have descended

KATMAI NATIONAL PARK

The ancient homeland of North American Eskimos was Alaska, including the rivers and forests of the southern part of the state. From there Eskimo populations spread eastward across Canada to Greenland in at least two major prehistoric expansions.

Katmai National Park lies at the base of the Alaska Peninsula. The park was created around the spectacular volcanos of this part of the Aleutian Range. However, archaeologists have discovered that this area was also an important crossroads for prehistoric Eskimos. The peninsula reaches out to the southwest, eventually turning into the Aleutian Island chain, home of the Eskimos' cousins, the Aleuts. To the southeast lies Kodiak Island. By crossing the peninsula through what is now the national park, early Eskimos could find food in either the Pacific Ocean or the Bering Sea.

Archaeologists working in Katmai National Park have found evidence of slowly changing Eskimo use of the region. Permafrost, the permanently frozen layer of soil just below the sod, has been both a blessing and a curse to their studies. Artifacts and food remains that would perish in a warmer climate are often preserved in and below the permafrost. Digging through the frozen ground, however, is slow and difficult. Long periods of exposure to warming Arctic sunlight are often required before excavation can proceed.

Early bands of Arctic hunters were probably in the Katmai area by 3000 B.C.. By the second millenium B.C. the prehistoric Eskimos of Katmai were using tools of the Arctic Small Tool tradition and living in well-built pit houses. The forest provided timber for roofs; fuel for fires; and beavers, bears, and caribou for food. Rivers were filled with salmon during the summer, and the waters off the nearby coasts yielded catches of waterfowl and sea mammals.

In this comparatively rich environment, early Eskimos could live in nearly permanent houses. Later, their fixed home bases would allow them to produce and accumulate pottery along with a broad range of tools made from stone, bone, and ivory. The cultural sequence uncovered by archaeologists at Katmai continues into the historic period. Visitors to the park can view reconstructed Eskimo houses and fish in the rich streams that fed Eskimo families for 5,000 years.

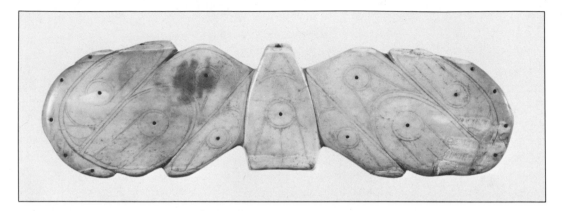

This bird-shaped piece carved of walrus ivory is from St. Lawrence Island, Alaska, south of the Bering Strait and close to the coast of Siberia. It is 21 centimeters (about 8 ¼ inches) long. Archaeologists are not sure of how it was used, but many believe that it may have been attached to a harpoon.

from either the older Northern Archaic tradition or some other source is still unknown. Slate tools and the knowledge of how to make them might have been spread either by population movements or from communication along the coast. The issue is important because the way in which toolmaking spread in this region may help us to understand the development of several Indian cultures farther south along the coast. If the spread of culture along the Northwest Coast after 2500 B.C. was carried by people moving south and east, then archaeologists might have to look for the ancestors of these people in Asia. If major population movements were not involved, then their ancestors are to be found among the Indians already present in North America before that time.

The new tradition that appeared in northern Alaska around 2500 B.C. is marked by a distinctive tool assemblage known as the Arctic Small Tool tradition. Tools of this tradition included tiny microblades, designed as cutting edges to be inserted into bone, ivory, or wooden shafts to make larger composite tools. Once again the origins of this new tradition appear to lie in Siberia. This tradition developed and spread quickly through the coastal Arctic zone, from the base of the Alaska Peninsula eastward to Greenland. The tradition did not move into the Aleutian Islands, and the Aleuts were not part of this development. The sites that characterize this tradition do not contain the oil lamps that would identify historic Eskimo cultures, so these early people must have depended on wood for light and heat. Although they lived near the coast and might be expected to have had snow igloos like those of recent Eskimos, their houses needed wood for both construction and heating, things that more recent Eskimos got along without. Because of their dependence on wood, the people of the Arctic Small Tool tradition could never move very far from the northern interior forests.

Many archaeologists have assumed that the Arctic Small Tool tradition was carried by people who spoke early Eskimo langauges. This theory has recently been put in doubt by researchers who point out that these people might have spoken a language unrelated to any other in North America, one that perhaps became extinct in the face of later Eskimo expansion across the region. In short, the bearers of the Arctic Small Tool tradition might have been early Eskimos, or they might have been something else, and it might never be know for sure.

The Arctic Small Tool tradition diversified as it spread eastward. Its descendants in Canada are known as Pre-Dorset. In Greenland they are called Sarqaq. These cultures were in place by 1900 B.C., and in some regions they lasted until 800 B.C. These descendants of the Arctic Small Tool tradition did not survive until historic times, thus it is uncertain whether or not they spoke true Eskimo languages.

After 1000 B.C. the Arctic Small Tool tradition moved more and more toward the use of marine resources, especially sea mammals. Later sites show larger amounts of bones from these animals. The change began as early as 1600 B.C. in northern Alaska, where Norton and related cultures known as Choris and Ipiutak have been identified. In addition, Old Whaling culture, whose artifacts are stylistically unlike those of any other culture, appeared suddenly in northwestern Alaska during this period and then disappeared a century later. It might have been brought by a temporary expansion of people from Siberia.

Stone implements from Sarquq, a pre-Dorset culture.

There was less diversity south of the Bering Strait, where only Norton culture is found at the Norton site and others like it. The carriers of Norton culture made crude pottery like their Siberian relatives, hunted sea mammals, and were almost certainly early Eskimos. Their Aleut relatives continued their own development through this period in isolation. The tools and food bones found in their site assemblages increasingly differ from what is found at the same time on the Alaskan mainland.

Meanwhile, in the eastern Arctic, Dorset culture emerged from Pre-Dorset in both Canada and Greenland. Dorset hunters also depended on marine mammals, especially seals and walrus. Bows and arrows, bones of domesticated dogs, and small stone lamps are sometimes found at Dorset sites, but there is none of the crude pottery that archaeologists find in Alaskan Norton culture sites. Whalebone snow-cutting knives for the construction of snow igloos, kayaks, ice creepers, and other tools typical of later Eskimo cultures also turn up in Dorset sites. Strangely, dogs, bows and arrows, and drills later disappeared from Dorset culture. Perhaps the hunting of sea mammals increased in importance, and equipment used to hunt land animals was simply abandoned.

In northern Alaska, Birnirk culture developed out of Norton culture after A.D. 500; it in turn evolved into Thule Eskimo culture over the course of the next few centuries. Thule culture was adopted by the other Eskimo communities in Alaska and spread rapidly eastward across northern Canada by around A.D. 1000. The Thule Eskimo replaced the Dorset culture, which had evolved out of the earlier Arctic Small Tool tradition. Perhaps the Dorset people died out because they lost out to the technologically superior Thule in the competition for Arctic resources. Perhaps they were absorbed by the expanding, dominant Thule culture. Whether the Dorset people spoke some early form of Eskimo or some non-Eskimo language, by the time of the first historic contacts, Eskimo speech from Greenland to northern Alaska was composed of dialects of a single widespread Eskimo language.

Thule Eskimos were indeed well equipped technologically for life in the far north. They had large open boats called umiaks, fleets of smaller, covered boats known as kayaks, the bow and arrow, an advanced type of dog sled, sophisticated harpoons, whale-oil lamps, snow igloos, and dozens of specialized gadgets made of stone, bone, ivory, sinew, copper, skin, and whatever other materials they could find. Modern versions of all of these items except the snow igloos are still in regular use in the Arctic, only slightly changed from their prehistoric counterparts. The Thule Eskimos' rich technology made expansion possible by enabling them to exploit more resources in more parts of the Arctic than had been possible for the Dorset. In addition, improved climate made expansion attractive allowing the supply of game

The earliest pictures of Eskimos to be seen in Europe were these drawings done in 1577 by John White, a member of Martin Frobisher's expedition to Baffin Island. White was the first European artist to record the plants, animals, and people native to North America. He later became governor of the English colony at Roanoke, Virginia, and made many drawings of Indian life in that area.

to increase and drawing the Eskimos into regions that in other periods might have been too forbidding even for the capable Thule people. The same warmer conditions that drew the Norse from Scandinavia west across the North Atlantic into the eastern Arctic around A.D. 1000 drew the Thule Eskimos to settle there as well. The two cultures would eventually clash in Greenland and Newfoundland, and the Norse would retreat back to Iceland from these North American outposts. Eskimo culture won out because it was better able to survive the return of cooler conditions. After this brief trial, European expansion into the Americas would be postponed for 500 years. ▲

Students excavate an archaic Indian site in Connecticut.

THE
CONQUEST
OF
AMERICA

Europeans began probing west across the Atlantic more than a thousand years ago, but their earliest efforts to explore and colonize were not very successful. Iceland was settled by Norse from Scandinavia beginning around A.D. 874. Later these people extended their settlements from Iceland to Greenland around 986. Their two Greenland settlements faced westward rather than back toward Europe. By A.D. 1000 further exploration had led to the establishment of at least one settlement in Vinland, as the Norse called the area west of their Greenland settlements. This was at the site of L'Anse aux Meadows, on the northern tip of what is now Newfoundland. Archaeologists found and began exploring the remains of Norse houses at this site only recently, so much work remains to be done. The settlement lasted only a few years until about 1013, when attacks by Indians, Eskimos, or both drove the Norse back to Greenland. The weather conditions, which had warmed and allowed the Norse to colonize Greenland in the first

place, cooled slowly after this, so the Greenland colonies also died out long before Columbus made his famous voyage. But stories of Norse explorers came down to later Europeans as fascinating rumors. Basque, Breton, Portuguese, English, and French fishermen might have known of America, but if they did they did not publicize it. So when Columbus sailed from Spain in 1492 he was looking for a trade route to Asia, not a new continent. John Cabot's 1497 voyage from England to Newfoundland also started as a search for Asia.

At the beginning of the 16th century, Europeans thought that the explorers really had found Asia, or at least some islands close to Asia. Navigation instruments at the time gave mariners a fairly good idea of their locations north or south of the equator, but not a clear idea of how far west they had gone. Not knowing exactly where they were and sometimes fearing the "Indians" they saw on shore, many explorers did little more than sail along the coast. For a hundred years after Co-

A reconstructed Norse house at L'Anse aux Meadows, Newfoundland, where there was a Norse settlement around A.D. 1000.

lumbus, only a few adventurous Spanish explorers led land expeditions into North America. The principal land explorations were made by Hernando de Soto (1539–43), Francisco Vásquez de Coronado (1540–42), and Álvar Núñez Cabeza de Vaca (1529–36).

Europeans did not take the idea of establishing colonies in America very seriously until many years after Columbus's discovery. Spanish explorers such as Hernán Cortés and Francisco Pizarro had found treasure in America in the 16th century, and most others at the time were mainly seeking the same

kinds of rewards. Early English and French outposts along the coast during this period were set up mainly as bases from which to raid Spanish treasure ships, which were filled with gold and silver from Mexico and Peru. Spanish coastal outposts were created mainly to protect their treasure-bearing ships. Sometimes missionaries came to America intending to remain and convert Indians to Christianity, but most explorers were interested mainly in returning home with riches.

Eventually Europeans discovered that America was an excellent source of furs. Beaver pelts were particularly popular—the long hairs of fur shaved from the pelts were used to make the large floppy men's felt hats fashionable in the mid-16th century. Furs were not of much interest to treasure hunters, so the fur trade began as a sideline for fishermen. Basque, Breton, Portuguese, English, and French fishermen made heavy use of the fishing waters off North America by this time.

Fishing boats from southern Europe carried salt from sources in the Mediterranean to cure fish on board and needed to land only to take on water and food. However, northern Europeans did not have cheap salt and had to preserve their catch by drying it. In order to do this, they constructed land stations on the coast of America. These fishermen apparently discovered that they could make an additional profit by trading with Indians at these locations, and so the fur trade began. By the time of Samuel de Champlain, Henry Hudson, and the other explorers of the early 17th century, European travelers and Indians living along the coast knew what they could sell and what they could get in exchange.

Syndics of the Drapers' Guild, *painted by Rembrandt in 1662. Hats made of beaver-fur felt became popular in Europe in the 16th century and would be a major motivation for trade between European nations and American Indians for two centuries.*

The record of European exploration in North America is very incomplete. It is clear that Europeans and Indians had important contacts with each other in at least half of the years of the 16th century. Some of the better-known cases deserve mention. Giovanni da Verrazano, an Italian working for the French, explored the Atlantic coast from Carolina northward in the summer of 1524. He landed and made contact with Indians at several places. Pánfilo de Narváez, who had been sent by the first Spanish governor of Cuba to bring Cortés back from Mexico eight years earlier, attempted to explore Florida in 1528. He took his men ashore at Tampa Bay and then lost contact with his ships. They walked westward along the coast to northwestern Florida. There they built new boats and took to the sea again. They continued westward until their boats were wrecked by a storm near modern-day Galveston, Texas. Narváez and most of his men drowned, but one boat made it to shore. The survivors, led by Álvar Núñez Cabeza de Vaca, then began what would be a seven-year hike across the deserts of Texas and northern Mexico. They eventually found their way to a Spanish outpost in western Mexico in 1536.

Meanwhile, the French explorer Jacques Cartier had made his first voyage to Canada in 1534. His second voyage stretched over the following two years, but his attempt to set up a colony at the site of modern-day Quebec did not succeed. Hernando de Soto began his journey into the Southeast in 1539,

and the Coronado expedition began the following year, thus in 1541 there were two major Spanish expeditions in North America. At the same time, Cartier was launching his third voyage to the Northeast. He returned to France the following year, and at the same time the Coronado expedition returned to Mexico after having come within only a few hundred miles of the de Soto expedition.

From 1549 on there were various French and Spanish attempts to establish posts along the coast of Florida and the Carolinas. French Protestants founded the settlement of Charlesfort on Parris Island, South Carolina, in 1562 and the more substantial Fort Caroline on the St. Johns River of northeast Florida two years later. In 1565, the Spanish captured the French settlements, executed the French they captured, and established the Spanish settlements of St. Augustine, San Mateo, and Santa Elena. The first of these survives as an archaeological site within a modern city on the northeast Florida coast.

Some European explorers crossed the Atlantic in search of the so-called Northwest Passage to Asia. The Dutch Martin Frobisher looked first in 1576 and led two more voyages in the following two years. In 1579, Sir Francis Drake crossed the Atlantic, sailed down the east coast of South America and up the west, going north past Mexico to explore the California coast. He then sailed westward across the Pacific on his trip around the world. In 1586, Fran-

Sir Walter Raleigh brought tobacco to England from Virginia. Tobacco was used by American Indians during ceremonies for healing and as a stimulant. In this illustration, Sir Walter is smoking; his servant, thinking him on fire, dashes into the room carrying water to pour onto the flames.

cis Drake returned to Florida to destroy Spanish St. Augustine.

Sir Walter Raleigh tried to establish an English colony at Roanoke, Virginia, in 1585, but the settlement was abandoned the following year. Raleigh sent settlers to Roanoke again in 1587. The Portuguese Vincente Gonzales saw evidence of the Roanoke colony when he explored Chesapeake Bay in 1588, but the colony's governor, John White, who had gone to England for supplies, found no trace of the settlers when he retuned to Virginia in 1590. The famous colony had mysteriously disappeared, leaving further searching to modern archaeologists. They have found some artifacts left by the colony, which are on display at Fort Raleigh National Historic Site, but the actual location of the village at Roanoke has yet to be uncovered.

Contacts between Europeans and Indians in the 16th century were not very numerous. There were two major expeditions inland, but most contacts took place at trading sites and a few settlements along the coast. Even so, this was the period in which trade goods began to flow in both directions, and the cultures of the two continents began to influence and change each other in many small ways. Europeans learned how to grow and use Indian tobacco, corn, beans, sunflowers, squash, and many other plants. Indians learned how to use iron tools, including, eventually, guns and gunpowder. The commonplace furs of North America were traded for equally commonplace glass beads and brass pots from Europe, and each partner considered that it was getting luxury goods at bargain prices.

Unfortunately, European contact brought epidemic diseases as well. The large range of domesticated animals in the Old World had contributed to the

In the spring, American Indians tapped maple trees to draw out the sap, which they boiled to make a sweet syrup. This early-17th-century drawing was made in Europe based on travelers' descriptions. Maple syrup and honey were the only sweeteners the Indians had.

development of many infectious diseases there. The spread of diseases such as bubonic plague, smallpox, and measles, often called "crowd infections," was promoted by dense populations. By 1492 these diseases were well established in European cities. But in America Indian populations had no previous exposure to such diseases and succumbed to them quickly. Epidemics of smallpox were particularly devastating. Although warfare did take a terrible toll, the conquest of North American Indians was accomplished largely by the spread of European diseases ahead of colonization. An unknown disease wiped out most Indian villages in coastal Massachusetts shortly before the Pilgrim settlers arrived. Elsewhere smallpox and other diseases frequently reduced Indian populations by as much as 90 percent, opening the land for European expansion and guaranteeing slight and ineffectual resistance in many places. At the same time economic pressures and religious and political conflicts in Europe brought people from there and Africa across the Atlantic in large numbers.

In the centuries following 1600 North America became filled with people of mainly European and African ancestry, speaking languages primarily of western European origin. Today Indian communities survive as minorities, often speaking English, French, or Spanish in addition to or instead of their traditional languages. Were it not for the diseases of the 16th and 17th centuries, people in North America might today be speaking Mohawk, Ojibwa, and Nahuatl and living their lives according to Native American rather than European customs.

Without European expansion and devastating epidemics, the largest archaeological sites of North America in the 16th century might be large native urban centers, probably located mostly along the tributaries of the Mississippi. But fate caused the most important sites of that century to be those of foreigners, placed along the edges of America. The Spanish settlement of St. Augustine continues to yield important archaeological information about the nature of Spanish colonial architecture and the effects of trade and intermarriage with local Timucua Indians. Elsewhere in the Southeast, archaeologists are successfully tracking the route of de Soto and his men. They recently found a piece of Spanish armor in one of the sites on his route.

Archaeologists have long sought the French colonial outposts of Cartier and others. The evidence of Cartier may be forever lost under modern Montreal, but traces of other French sites have occasionally been found and preserved. The small French and Spanish forts along the Carolina coast have been studied extensively and many are now open to tourists.

The early English settlements of Jamestown, Virginia, and Plymouth, Massachusetts, are both substantially reconstructed, and both places have im-

(continued on page 130)

EPIDEMICS AND DEPOPULATION

Most of the worst diseases that afflict humans appear to have developed first in one or another of the nonhuman animal species that inhabit the earth. Most of them also depend upon densely populated human communities to survive and spread as epidemics. Such conditions existed from very early times in Europe, Asia, and Africa. The prehistoric peoples on those continents had access to many animal species that were suitable for domestication (and were potential sources for the development of diseases). Consequently, animal husbandry is thousands of years old in the Eastern Hemisphere, and this in turn helped in the development of agriculture and the rise of dense urban populations. The Indians of the Americas, however, were not in contact with such animal species. They developed agriculture and became urbanized later, and to a lesser extent.

Domesticated animals and urban life appear to have given Old World people a significant advantage, but these blessings were mixed. Before modern sanitation systems were built, urban populations were generally less healthy than their tribal ancestors. Any new disease could spread rapidly.

Indians tend the sick during an epidemic. The traditional Indian remedies—the use of heat and smoke or sucking to draw out the presumed source of the illness—did not help and actually made many sick people worse. This drawing, made in Europe in the 1570s, was based on travelers' descriptions of South American Indian life.

Further, their close proximity to both domesticated and undomesticated animals allowed relatively harmless diseases to jump in mutated, or genetically changed, forms into the human population. The worst epidemic of all for Europeans was a disease of the black rat that became the dreaded bubonic plague. The Black Death, as it was also called, killed two-thirds to three-fourths of all Europeans in the 13th century. The surviving population countered the rising death rates of this and later waves of the plague with higher birth rates.

Cowpox also entered the European human population, where it became known as smallpox. Europeans adjusted to this horrible disease as well and carried it with them to the Americas.

American Indians had little experience with domesticated animals and urban life. When smallpox reached their shores, starting in the 16th century, it spread rapidly and widely, reducing local populations by proportions equivalent to those that had been inflicted by the Black Death in Europe three centuries earlier. Eventually the American Indians adjusted to the new disease load, but as in Europe it took a long time. Only now, several centuries after they were stricken by the epidemics, are the populations of American Indians returning to their A.D. 1492 levels.

Smallpox and other diseases struck first where Europeans landed first, in the islands of the Caribbean. These diseases spread into Mexico shortly after the Spanish conquest. Other parts of North America escaped until European settlement expanded a century or two later. Some Indian nations were decimated, and several communities wiped out entirely. In eastern Massachusetts, for example, an epidemic around 1616 took the lives of almost all of the inhabitants of a Patuxet Wampanoag village, literally clearing the way for the Pilgrims to occupy the same site four years later. In some other places 80 or 90 percent of the population died.

The speed with which disease spread and the death rates that followed are matters of dispute among scientists. These issues are important because often the only population statistics existing for Indian nations date from after the first or second wave of disease. Until we better understand the spread and severity of epidemics, we will have only archaeology to tell us how many Indians there were on the continent at the time of Columbus's voyage. Archaeological evidence can help us to understand the settlement patterns of those early populations—the number and sizes of villages and how the population was distributed in the varied environments across the continent. We can now be fairly sure that there were more than 2 million people north of Mexico in 1492, but depending upon the results of future research the final estimate could be two or three times that many. Much new investigation of the few written documents we have, plus additional archaeology and analysis by computers, will be necessary to resolve the current controversy.

Towana Spivey (left), an archaeologist who is an American Indian, supervises excavations at Fort Towson in southeastern Oklahoma. The dig produced prehistoric Caddo (Mississippian) artifacts as well as those made by historic Choctaw people, along with military materials from the 19th-century fort.

(continued from page 127)

portant archaeological programs. As is the case at most sites of this era, the interaction of European and Indian cultures is an important focus of archaeological research. What has been found supports the view that in the early years the people of these cultures, each alien to the other, usually interacted more or less as equals. Each learned from, borrowed from, and stole from the other, often giving (or losing) as much in return.

Even without the spread of epidemics, the Indian cultures of North America were at a disadvantage in the face of European expansion. Europe was at the core of a growing world economic system, and its spread through colonization was promoted by large and well-organized nations of a type that had not yet developed in North America. The nations of North America still lacked many of the features of state organizations such as permanent bureau-

WORKING IN ARCHAEOLOGY

The practice of archaeology started out as a treasure hunt, and most modern archaeologists have to admit that the excitement of discovery was a strong attraction when they first began. Today exciting archaeological discoveries come out of computers as well as out of the ground. Good archaeology has come to depend more and more upon teamwork and expensive equipment. An individual with a shovel can no longer carry out a proper excavation alone regardless of how skilled and careful he or she may be. Years of study and specialized training are now required.

Archaeological resources are irreplaceable. The evidence of American Indian prehistory disappears daily through careless excavation as well as unintentional destruction by the construction of dams, roads, and other facilities. We know that we cannot always preserve archaeological finds in museums as well as they would have been preserved if we had simply left them undisturbed in the ground. We are also aware that methods and techniques we have not yet developed will undoubtedly be better than those we now have available. At the same time, many sites facing certain destruction need quick and careful investigation. These and other considerations have changed the character of archaeological research in recent years. Private treasure hunting is strongly discouraged and often illegal. Even major universities must carefully justify archaeological excavation and demonstrate that they have the proper equipment, qualified participants, and adequate storage facilities before undertaking fieldwork.

Despite growing restrictions on archaeological fieldwork, there are more opportunities for participation now than in the past. Nearly every state has a statewide archaeological society, often with local chapters. State societies are usually for people primarily interested in American Indian archaeology. The Archaeological Institute of America began with interests primarily in classical (Greek, Roman, and Near Eastern) archaeology but in recent years has expanded its interests. Archaeology clubs have also sprung up in both junior and senior high schools. All of these organizations often have close ties with colleges, universities, and museums. Beginners can often find volunteer positions on sponsored excavations and in established laboratories. Workers with more experience are often paid by public and private organizations involved in salvaging important archaeological sites. Some go on to advanced study and take up careers in archaeology.

Although archaeology is still not a large profession, there are challenging positions available for those who have the interest and might have the talent. There are careers for those with ability and opportunities for those looking only for part-time participation. Much of the past remains to be uncovered.

cracies and standing armies. The collapse of Indian populations surely sped the process, but anthropologists are still trying to determine whether or not conquest was inevitable.

For a long time American archaeology has involved transplanted Europeans or their descendants as scholars and American Indians as subjects. Fortunately, this situation has begun to change as some Indians have become archaeologists and some non-Indian sites have become the subjects of excavation. Archaeology in North America has special significance for people of American Indian descent. Indians are sometimes members of field crews, and their non-Indian co-workers envy the special meaning that they derive from uncovering the prehistory of North America.

Unfortunately, people calling themselves archaeologists have angered both Indians and legitimate archaeolo-

Archaeology students help to clean up a site in Union County, Kentucky, where artifact hunters dug into and desecrated about 450 Indian graves. The students are sifting dirt to recover bone fragments for reburial.

Robert Thomas, a Shawnee Indian from Oklahoma, offers tobacco to the spirits of Indian ancestors before their graves were reconsecrated. Standing on the site of the desecrated graves in Union County, Kentucky, he offered tobacco on each of the four days before the reburial took place on Memorial Day, 1988.

gists by looting burials and other sites for fun and profit. Even professional archaeologists have sometimes contributed to misunderstanding by showing less sensitivity toward Indian burial sites than they would toward their own. These difficulties are being resolved as professional archaeology grows and Indians become more directly involved in it.

Most modern Americans are the descendants of immigrants from other parts of the world, heirs to the explorers of the 16th century. The idea of archaeology came from Europe, and most of the Americans who practice archaeology have been of European descent. For all of us, whatever our personal origin, American Indian archaeology is interesting for scientific and humanistic reasons. Some of our findings will surely have unexpected significance for future generations, for that is always the case in the sciences. ▲

BIBLIOGRAPHY

Claiborne, Robert. *The First Americans*. New York: Time-Life Books, 1973.

Collins, Henry B., et al. *The Far North: 2,000 Years of American Eskimo and Indian Art*. Bloomington: Indiana University Press, 1973.

Deetz, James. *Invitation to Archaeology*. New York: Doubleday, 1967.

Dockstader, Frederick J. *Indian Art in America: The Arts and Crafts of the North American Indian*. Greenwich, CT: Museum of the American Indian Press, 1967.

Drucker, Phillip. *Cultures of the North Pacific Coast*. San Francisco: Harper & Row, 1965.

Dutton, Bertha P. *American Indians of the Southwest*. Albuquerque: University of New Mexico Press, 1983.

Fagan, Brian. *The Great Journey: The Peopling of Ancient America*. New York: Thames and Hudson, 1987.

Holm, Bill. *Northwest Coast Indian Art: An Analysis of Form*. Seattle: University of Washington Press, 1965.

Leone, Mark P., ed. *Contemporary Archaeology: A Guide to Theory and Contributions*. Carbondale: Southern Illinois University Press, 1972.

Scherer, Joanna C. *Indians: The Great Photographs that Reveal North American Indian Life 1847–1929*. New York: Crown, 1974.

Snow, Dean R. *Foundation of Northeast Archaeology: A Guide to Theory and Contributions*. Carbondale: Southern Illinois University Press, 1972.

————. *Native American Prehistory: A Critical Bibliography*. Bloomington: Indiana University Press, 1980.

Snow, Dean R., and Werner Forman. *The Archaeology of North America*. New York: Viking, 1976.

Tamarin, Alfred, and Shirley Glubock. *Ancient Indians of the Southwest*. New York: Doubleday, 1975.

Thomas, David Hurst. *Archaeology*. New York: Holt, Rinehart and Winston, 1972.

Willey, Gordon R., and Jeremy Sabloff. *A History of American Archaeology*. San Francisco: Freeman, 1974.

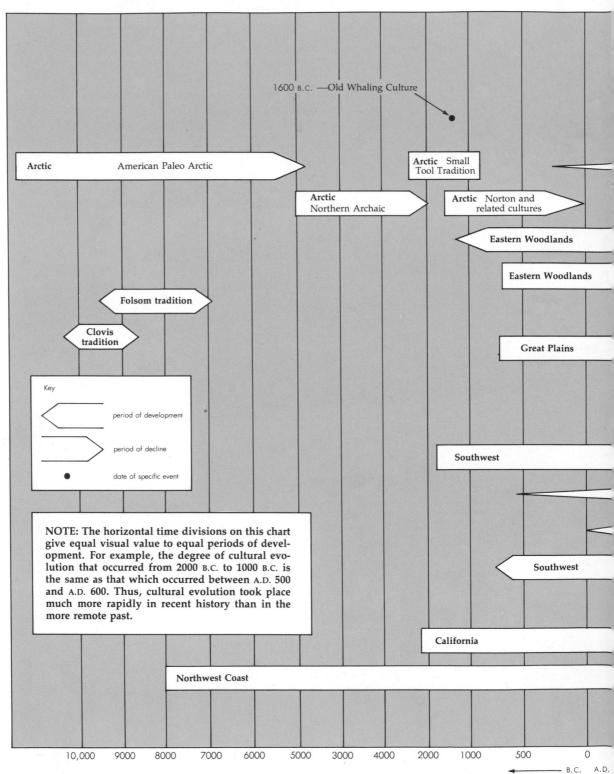

1600 B.C. —Old Whaling Culture

Arctic   American Paleo Arctic

Arctic Small Tool Tradition

Arctic
Northern Archaic

Arctic Norton and related cultures

Eastern Woodlands

Eastern Woodlands

Folsom tradition

Great Plains

Clovis
tradition

Key

period of development

period of decline

● date of specific event

Southwest

NOTE: The horizontal time divisions on this chart give equal visual value to equal periods of development. For example, the degree of cultural evolution that occurred from 2000 B.C. to 1000 B.C. is the same as that which occurred between A.D. 500 and A.D. 600. Thus, cultural evolution took place much more rapidly in recent history than in the more remote past.

Southwest

California

Northwest Coast

10,000 9000 8000 7000 6000 5000 3000 4000 2000 1000 500 0

← B.C.   A.D.

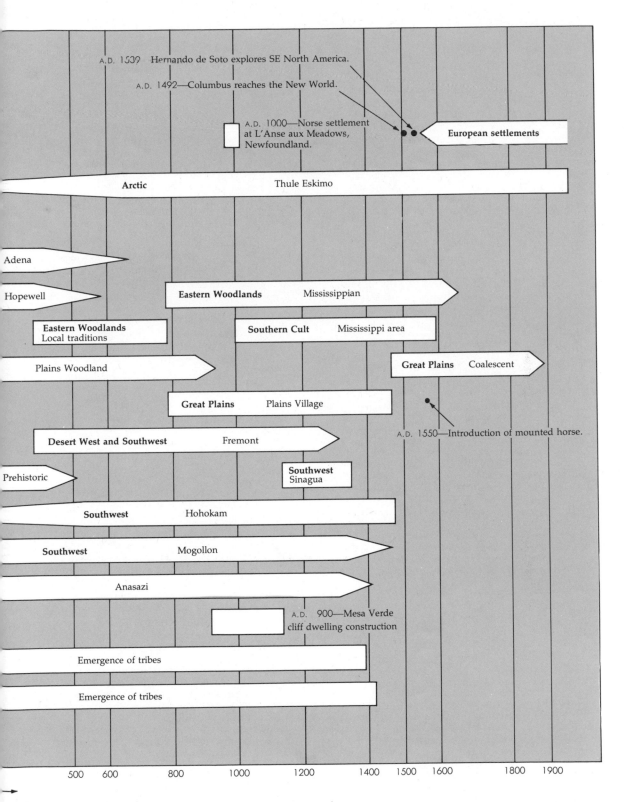

A.D. 1539—Hernando de Soto explores SE North America.

A.D. 1492—Columbus reaches the New World.

A.D. 1000—Norse settlement at L'Anse aux Meadows, Newfoundland.

European settlements

Arctic   Thule Eskimo

Adena

Hopewell

Eastern Woodlands   Mississippian

Eastern Woodlands Local traditions

Southern Cult   Mississippi area

Plains Woodland

Great Plains   Coalescent

Great Plains   Plains Village

Desert West and Southwest   Fremont

A.D. 1550—Introduction of mounted horse.

Southwest Sinagua

Prehistoric

Southwest   Hohokam

Southwest   Mogollon

Anasazi

A.D. 900—Mesa Verde cliff dwelling construction

Emergence of tribes

Emergence of tribes

500   600   800   1000   1200   1400 1500 1600   1800 1900

137

GLOSSARY

adobe A building material or brick made of sun-dried earth and straw.

adze A stone implement usually made by grinding rather than chipping; used by prehistoric American Indians for gouging and preparing timbers. See also *celt.*

anthropology The study of the physical, social, and cultural characteristics of human beings. Sub-disciplines include archaeology, ethnology, biological anthropology, and linguistics.

Archaic cultures North American Indian ways of life that developed after the end of the Ice Age and generally before the use of pottery, cultivated plants, and permanent villages. Some evolved into more advanced cultures thousands of years ago, while others remained relatively simple until the 19th century.

Archaic Period The period from about 10,000 to 3,000 B.P., when people in North America began using stone and bone tools and obtained food by hunting and gathering. It was generally characterized by seasonal migrations and the use of fire and showed effective use of local natural resources.

artifact Any object made by human beings, such as a tool, garment, dwelling, or ornament. Also, any marking in or on the earth indicating the previous existence of such an object. The artifacts generally found by archaeologists may have been lost or deliberately left behind.

atlatl Aztec word for spear-thrower, an implement used to extend the length of a hunter's throwing arm and thereby add force and distance to the throw. Spear-throwers were in general use in North America until they were largely replaced by the bow and arrow around 2,000 years ago.

burial mounds See *mound.*

celt A stone ax head usually made by grinding rather than chipping; used by prehistoric American Indians for heavy-duty woodworking. See also *adze.*

chert A glassy stone from which flakes can be removed by hammering or pressure. It was the preferred material for chipped stone tool manufacture in much of prehistoric North America. Chert occurs naturally in many limestone and shale deposits.

chronology The arrangement of objects, dates, or sites in order of their occurrence in time.

clan A multigenerational group having a shared identity, organization, and property, based on belief in descent from a common totemic (mythic) ancestor. Because clan members consider themselves closely related, marriage within the clan is strictly prohibited.

culture The learned behavior of human beings; non-biological, socially taught activities; the way of life of a given group of people.

dendrochronology A precise dating technique involving the patterns and spacing of tree rings preserved in wood samples from archaeological sites.

earthwork Burial mound, temple mound, or other large structure built of earth. Most prehistoric earthworks in North America are found in the Eastern Woodlands and the prairies.

fluted point A projectile point of the Paleo-Indian Period made by removing long "channel" flakes from the sides to thin out the base of the point. This allowed the point to be securely fastened to the spear.

graver Ground or chipped stone tool designed to incise or engrave materials softer than stone, such as bone or wood.

horticulture Food production using human muscle power and simple hand tools to plant and harvest domesticated crops.

Ice Age A time in the earth's past when vast ice sheets or glaciers expanded to cover much of North America and Eurasia, and periodically retreated and advanced again. The most recent Ice Age began about 18,000 years ago and ended about 10,000 years ago.

kiva An underground chamber in the pueblos of the Indians of the Southwest, where men held secret ceremonies. The kivas of the Pueblo Indians are probably derived from the partly underground homes in which earlier people of the region lived. See *pit house.*

knapping The technique of stone tool manufacture through careful chipping, using both hammer blows and pressure techniques.

matrilineal descent; matrilineality A way of figuring family or clan membership by tracing kinship through female ancestors.

medicine wheel Any of several known prehistoric circular arrangements of boulders in the High Plains, presumed to have astronomical and ceremonial significance.

mound A large earthen construction built by prehistoric American Indians as a substructure for a public building or to contain human graves.

moundbuilders The prehistoric builders of earthen mounds, once thought to be a lost race but now known to be the ancestors of modern American Indians.

Paleo-Indian Period The period in North America lasting until about 10,000 years ago, when human lifeways involved hunting large mammals and making specialized stone tools.

Paleolithic The Old Stone Age of the Eastern Hemisphere, during which human beings evolved to their modern form and which lasted until about 10,000 years ago, out of which came the earliest tool industries of Paleo-Indians.

patrilineal descent; patrilineality A way of figuring family or clan membership by tracing kinship through male ancestors.

pièces esquillés Small stone wedges used by Paleo-Indians for splitting and working antler and bone.

pit house A dwelling built into an excavation in the ground; may be partially or completely underground.

Pleistocene See *Ice Age.*

projectile points Stone weapon tips that were attached to wooden shafts to form spears, lances, and arrows.

radiocarbon dating Method for determining the approximate age of ancient objects based on the known rate of decay of radioactive carbon. This form of carbon, which occurs in predictable amounts in plants and animals, begins to decay when the organism dies.

reservation, reserve A tract of land set aside by treaty for Indian occupation and use, often without the consent of the Indians themselves.

residential patterns The stains or other signs left in the ground by human settlements of every kind, from small temporary camps to large permanent cities. Such patterns provide information about the cultural systems that left them.

sipapu A hole in the floor of a Southwestern kiva or pit house, symbolizing the hole in the earth through which the mythological ancestors of Anasazi Indians emerged into the world.

site Any location identified as having a concentration of artifacts or features resulting from past human use or habitation.

spear-thrower See *atlatl.*

spokeshave A chipped stone tool with a concave cutting edge that was used to shape and smooth wooden shafts; so called because of its similarity to iron tools used to shape wooden wagon spokes.

terracing The practice of shaping steep hill slopes into stepped fields to prevent rapid erosion of soil and loss of plants.

tool kit The set of artifact types typically carried and used by an individual in any particular prehistoric culture.

tradition A distinct way of life, usually restricted to a single region but often lasting for several centuries.

tundra The Arctic landscape of grasses and shrubs, the surface of which thaws every summer but which has a permanently frozen layer beneath the surface.

type site Any site regarded as the first or most typical example of a particular prehistoric culture or tradition. The names of type sites are customarily used to identify the larger culture or tradition.

weir A wooden fence or rock wall constructed in a stream to trap fish or force them into a narrow channel where they can easily be netted.

Woodland period The time when people in North America practiced horticulture, made pottery, used the bow and arrow, buried their dead in cemeteries marked by mounds of earth, and lived in permanent villages. This period lasted from about 10,000 to 3,000 years ago but varies slightly from region to region.

INDEX

PICTURE CREDITS

DEAN R. SNOW is a professor of anthropology at the State University of New York at Albany. He received his B.A. in anthropology from the University of Minnesota and his Ph.D. in anthropology from the University of Oregon. He is the author or coauthor of 8 books and more than 40 articles and book chapters, as well as a number of reviews and unpublished technical monographs. His books include *The Atlas of Ancient America* (1986, with Michael Coe and Elizabeth Benson), *The Archaeology of New England* (1981), and *The Archaeology of North America* (1976). His primary research and writing concerns are the archaeology and ethnohistory of the Iroquois.

FRANK W. PORTER III, general editor of INDIANS OF NORTH AMERICA, is director of the Chelsea House Foundation for American Indian Studies. He holds a B.A., M.A., and Ph.D. from the University of Maryland. He has done extensive research concerning the Indians of Maryland and Delaware and is the author of numerous articles on their history, archaeology, geography, and ethnography. He was formerly director of the Maryland Commission on Indian Affairs and American Indian Research and Resource Institute, Gettysburg, Pennsylvania, and he has received grants from the Delaware Humanities Forum, the Maryland Committee for the Humanities, the Ford Foundation, and the National Endowment for the Humanities, among others. Dr. Porter is the author of *The Bureau of Indian Affairs* in the Chelsea House KNOW YOUR GOVERNMENT series.